quarter passed:
collected works from twentysomethings around the world

Quarter Passed

collected works from twentysomethings
around the world

edited by vivek bidwai & larikus scott

twenty
stories
publishing

Copyright © 2009 by Twenty Stories Publishing, LLC

Book & Cover design by Katie Mahjoubi

All rights reserved. No part of this book may be reproduced in any form or by any electronic or mechanical means, including information storage and retrieval systems, without permission in writing from the publisher. The only exception is by a reviewer, who may quote short excerpts in a review.

Twenty Stories Publishing, LLC, Washington, District of Columbia
First Printing: March 2009

Library of Congress Control Number: 2008943484

ISBN-13 978-0-9799548-0-1
ISBN-10 0-9799548-0-0

Visit our website at
www.twentystories.com

Printed in the United States of America

10 9 8 7 6 5 4 3 2 1

for our families and friends

contents

introduction		
a note from the editors		xii
acknowledgments		xv

chapter 1: growing up

dawn ng, singapore	once upon a house	2
sara sky schutte, italy	no ride	13
morenike balogun, denmark	limbo	14
abdel munem amin, canada	stripped corridor	15
petra kristine turner, canada	insomnia	16
clarissa caldwell, united states	egg chalaza	18
	the goo inside	19
jonathan thomas, united states	untitled	23
stephan delbos, czech republic	fuel	24
ólöf jóhannsdóttir, iceland	herbergi	25
bridgette holmes, united states	mother	26
elvina trixie, china	fire and ice	28
rhiannon elston, australia	confession	29
meaghan e. doss, united states	fuck	30
dylan mark belden, united states	29	31
vishal shah, england	kids	35

chapter 2: tradition

aaron alper, united states	religious conflict	38

ruthie kott, united states	keeping the faith	39
ksenia shashounova, russia	untitled	43
lucy brydon, scotland	traveling riverside blues	44
laila antone habash, west bank	untitled	48
rebecca peacock, united states	my own woman	49
michelle hensarling, united states	my ohio	50
dana goldman, united states	quitting	52
ryan jernigan, united states	cold feet	55
bryan david blake, italy	in those years we lived our best	56
oluwagbemiga dasylva, nigeria	rhythm	64
alessandra mccune, united states	final 3	65

chapter 3: self image

katherine prengel, england	the smokers	68
albert chi hwang, united states	apollo	71
a.j. agnew, canada	for me	72
marina bendet, russia	twice	73
tracy bradley, canada	being poor	74
chris vialpando, united states	untitled	77
lucy leitner, united states	whiskey and fire	78
emily mae bezaire, united states	melencolia	87
gena mavuli, argentina	how to lighten a heavy load	88
laura elena soria pineda, mexico	untitled	90
vicky puzon-diopenes, thailand	dances with stars	91
corey podell, united states	happy anniversary	92
constanza fontenla, argentina	imagen	95

chapter 4: relationships & sexuality

sarah hamilton, canada	men / women	98
b.h. shepherd, united states	confessions of a southern hustler	99
chloe lewis, canada	kiss	107
phil groman, china	shining knight	108
donia lilly, greece	light and darkness	110
jayar pacifico, united states	gay… in a good way	111
karishma singh, india	crystal raindrop	123
owen austin, japan	deactivated ballad	124
maria gregoriou, cyprus	domestic discipline	125
tim martin, england	shelley croatia	126
amy bleu, united states	the red dress in the window	127
daniel davy, united states	mixing up	128
gina dunn, united states	lovers	133

chapter 5: loss & challenge

maya bastian, canada	simon	136
jessica darmanin, canada	walk the line	139
maria giuliani, canada	smile, buddy	140
mike foster, united states	despair	142
sharyn goldyn, united states	stupidest thing i've ever done	143
frederick bernas, england	belgrade shanty	147
artila devi, fiji	my life's education	148
joão machado, brazil	face in the cemetery	152
alanna davis-robins, united states	the incessant writings of an uneducated woman	153
archie p. valdez, united states	seclusion	160

kelley calvert, united states	no airplanes in the sky	161
adrianus smith, jr., namibia	sunset	167

chapter 6: career

sarah nelson, france	rejection	170
	the rejection collection	171
peter ryan, united states	nameless and faceless	173
dixon bordiano, united states	pilgrims	175
wade forrest wilson, canada	boiling milk	176
mike o'donnell, united states	last chance road	180
jessica watson, canada	ode to the office	181
carol j. thomas, panama	desempleo	182
maryam gerling salassi, united states	untitled	184
katherine chamberlain, united states	forgetting yourself	185
hava helan, poland	the mouth above my door	186
andrew blackman, england	tainted	188
patrick emery yurick, united states	off to work	193
brandon miree, united states	the first quarter	194

a note from the editors...

The twenties represent a constant balancing act, a period of developmental certainty and personal uncertainty. Standing before a vast expanse of life choices with varying outcomes - and consequences - during this critical formative decade can be both exhilarating and daunting. In recent years, a number of books and media outlets have raised key questions about the experiences of young men and women in their twenties. Some have called the struggles and successes of this decade symptoms of a quarter-life crisis; others have regarded this chapter of life as prolonged adolescence, accelerated middle age, and even as old age.

We embarked on this journey because we felt that most of our peers were not represented by the prevalent theories and prescribed self-help solutions, and we set out to compile works that would cross geographical, sexual, cultural, ideological, occupational and socioeconomic boundaries, and address the twenties in a new way.

A vast majority of prose, poetry, artwork and photography that we encounter and consume in popular culture is created by a dedicated minority of professional writers, artists and editors. Breaking into the inner circle of publishing has never been easy, particularly for individuals pursuing other careers.

Some of our contributors have never considered publishing their works before; dozens more told tales of editors who had been wary of publishing their "unproven" compositions; others lamented mainstream published content that rarely challenged time-honored norms or addressed relevant issues with new voices and perspectives.

When we began working on *Quarter Passed*, we had no budget, no publishing connections, and no formal experience to speak of. Rather than pursuing a traditional path with a conventional publishing company, we chose to establish a new kind of publisher and setup a forum for our peers to express themselves.

Twenty Stories Publishing allowed us to grow beyond the confines of 9-to-5 existences and reconnect with our own love of writing. As an independent publishing source, we looked beyond typical subsets of potential contributors and encouraged a wider audience of our peers to overcome real and perceived limitations in their own lives and in the publishing world.

We received nearly 1,500 creative compositions from 40 countries across 6 continents. From Barbados to the West Bank, the Philippines to Namibia, our contributors are chefs and bankers, optimists and pessimists, rich and poor. Although this volume represents 80 original works, we were unable to include countless other deserving pieces.

While we have made revisions for fluidity and cohesion, we have not attempted to create a single approach to editing the works contained herein. We have tried to be sensitive to differing schools of grammar and syntax and varying systems of rhythm and flow by leaving the integrity of each piece intact. Moreover, our team of editors has not attempted to assign meaning to the creative works in this book. Rather, each piece represents a single perspective at a critical life juncture.

Throughout the creative process, we searched for ways to present the selected works in a coherent, unified way. Sorting authors by age, sex or geographic location ran contrary to the underlying aim of the book. We purposely left our submission guidelines open, encouraging our peers to express their thoughts regarding any particular aspect of their twentysomething experience. Yet, as more and more works arrived, in spite of the widely-varying perspectives and demographics, several themes emerged and underscored relevant topics that every twentysomething faces.

The following core themes eventually came into focus: *growing up*, is less about aging and more about having the confidence to make difficult decisions and learn from both triumphs and failures; *tradition*, may refer to a culture, religion, belief or custom - but it is, above all, a piece of home that each of us carries; *self image*, is the lens through which we see ourselves in relation to the world; *relationships & sexuality*, are inherently private facets of life that have become increasingly visible, and which remain inextricably linked to our emotional well-being; *loss & challenge*, are inevitabilities that push us to dig deep in search of hope and the strength to persevere; *career*, refers to the path one chooses in life, not merely to job titles and tax brackets.

Considerable overlap exists between each of these themes, and most of the compositions of *Quarter Passed* span several categories. But part of enjoying the journey through this collection - and one's twenties, really - is realizing that there are no clear lines in the sand to delineate and compartmentalize experience.

At any age, it is easy to feel stifled, creatively, emotionally, professionally, philosophically, ideologically. Publishing this collection has been an exercise in self-expression, empowerment and community-building, and although we make no pretense at broad conclusions or statements about our generation, it is our hope that every reader is able to connect in some way with the creative works that follow.

V.B. and L.S.

acknowledgments

We would first and foremost like to thank the young writers, artists, poets and photographers who submitted their works to this project.

We would also like to thank our dedicated team of readers, editors and designers for volunteering countless hours to this book, and without whom it would never have been completed: Karnika Bhalla, Neeta Bidwai, Levee Brooks, Vanessa Chang, Shannon Gadley, George Hwang, Thomas Kim, Rusty MacMullan, Katie Mahjoubi, David Santiago, Carrie Scott, Rekha Shetty, Rebecca Vo, Kristen Wallerstedt, and Jessica Wilson.

Thanks as well to Andre Gary and Ron Gong (www.theappsource.com) for web development and support.

Lastly, thank you to our families and friends - for your enduring support and encouragement. Without you, this would not have been possible.

1

growing up

once upon a house

by dawn ng

a bedtime story for the anonymous American

once upon a house

For most five year-olds, a house looks like a fat square wearing a triangle hat. Add two smaller squares and a skinny rectangle to get two windows and a door. A creative child might throw in a bunch of squiggly lines around a circle to illustrate a sun with rays, a dog the size of a full-grown horse, and an open lawn with a single tree.

When I was five, my family lived twenty stories above the closest grass patch, which I could see whenever my father carried me out onto the balcony. We stayed in a 200 square meter flat on the east side of Singapore. And, although I had 1348 neighbors and no dog (and one albino hamster who put an early end to his cyclical existence by throwing himself against the spindle of his running wheel), I drew the same imaginary house as everyone else.

I should have drawn one long vertical rectangle with 500 or more tiny squares. But I must've seen this house on TV or in some storybook, because lethargically flapping from the Mitsubishi refrigerator in the kitchen was my bright Crayola masterpiece of this typical home, complete with bright green lawn and Godzilla retriever.

Every Sunday, my family had dinner at my grandmother's house. Like us, she also lived in a high-rise flat. Statistics reveal that more than 85 percent of Singaporeans do. Bobbing in the syrupy swelter of the equatorial sun, our island

quarter passed

is the size of a tiny dot on the world atlas but home to more than 4.3 million people. Because of this, land prices are exorbitant and most Singaporeans have no choice but to breathe, eat and sleep on top of each other.

Sunday was also my grandmother's mahjong day with her friends. The old ladies formed a noisy huddle around a small table in her apartment, their papery hands swirling flat, lacquered tiles with Chinese numerals. As casual chitchat drifted to the usual topic of grandchildren, all eyes would fall on my small body sprawled across the living room floor, where I lay clutching my crayons in front of the flickering TV.

"Yi kor ah, jiak gan tang," my grandmother declared.

Directly translated from Hokkien, a Chinese dialect, she meant, "That child eat potato." What it implied was that I didn't eat rice. Not literally, but that I was a prototype of my Happy Meal generation of young Westernized Singaporeans, who ran around in lit-up LA Gear sneakers screaming for someone to read us Dr. Seuss.

I was a foreigner to her in her own home, a stranger beneath my yellow skin. She often expressed this in different ways with different words, her voice ebbing between shame and pride. I was Version 4.0 of what she and my parents could've ever hoped to become: more educated, more privileged, more White.

My grandmother's mahjong companions usually clucked in sympathy. But as it was, in that living room, I was only five years old. And amidst the cacophony of clacking mahjong tiles and idle chit chat, I was too absorbed drawing your house on my drawing pad to notice.

apartment hunting

I left home on two significant solo occasions by the time I turned fifteen.

The first was a school geography field trip to England when I was fourteen. It was a month-long affair on a tour bus, which refused to dispatch us screaming girls at shopping districts in Liverpool and Bath. Instead, the bus made stops at various cliff formations and streams that dribbled across the outskirts of Engonce upon a house

land.

"This place looks like shit," my friend Shiying noted as she stared out at the streaks of grey farms and token sheep. We were both accustomed to superhighways and sun-scattering towers of concrete and glass. It was drizzling. England was always dank, dewy, humid, drenched, soggy or moist when we were there. When it wasn't wet, it was damp. It was as if someone above had left a dull rotating sprinkler on and forgot to turn it off.

"People here are ugly and everyone is at least sixty," Shiying grumbled, compressing her knees against the seat ahead of her. "No wonder Stamford Raffles sailed all the way over to colonize Singapore."

Though our blasé spirits underwent a remarkable lift when the tour bus pulled up at Oxford Street in London, the two of us were already set against one day attending college in this soggy country, which - we learned from history textbooks - ditched us when the Japanese invaded during World War II anyway. Instead, we talked excitedly of going to America. In America, everyone looks like Brad Pitt. In America, everyone has a Baywatch tan.

The second time I left home was a year later because I got a 53 on a math final. I can't recall the exact scream fest that unfolded with my mother, but I do remember telling her I'd had it with her damn expectations. I also took the opportunity to shed some light on a couple of solid facts:

1. I hated math;
2. I hated my math teacher, Miss Tan;
3. I hated this top school where math was so important;
4. I hated this country which depended on number-crunching human robots.

It was 11 p.m. and when I slammed the metal grill door of my flat, my mother shouted, "You want to go? You think you're so smart on your own? Good! Go! Don't come back!" After three hours of sitting under the deck with four stray cats and a mumbling old lady, I returned. It was my father who opened the door.

When he saw me, he hugged me and said, "Why did you make your mother cry?"

quarter passed

moving out

My family moved three times before I turned eighteen. If we had initially been considered part of Singapore's upper-middle social strata, my father succeeded in moving us closer to the crust. We now owned a landed property in a prime location on the southwest side of the island.

Growing up, I was fiercely competitive and, like most of the kids I knew, I was funneled into the best learning institutions. In class, we were argumentative, outspoken and bent on being successful in some way or other. And we all understood that the best way was to simply become a doctor, banker or lawyer.

No one explicitly told us this. Most of our parents brought us up flipping through Western guidebooks on how to raise children, and they were sufficiently convinced that kids should be given the prerogative to grow in the direction they pleased. For the most part, parents exercised patience, love and support unless one of us really crossed the line and decided to be an artist, or a pro bono-something.

By the time I was eighteen, the National Arts Council was set up in Singapore and Shakespeare became a compulsory fixture in secondary school curriculums. Two years later, a $900 million dazzling waterfront arts hub named "The Esplanade" was set to bring Sydney's Opera House to shame.

"Culture follows prosperity," people said. And now that Singapore had - in a single generation - vaulted from zinc-roof houses to skyscrapers, we could diversify and pursue our passions. As the world's twelfth richest economy, hell, we could even buy sophistication wholesale.

But I guess real changes aren't erected by proposals, committee boards and $900 million buildings. Real changes require a collective realignment of social attitudes and beliefs; a gradual turning of the tide which, even for the West, took generations to occur. Because of this, the ideological residue of my nation's Third World past continued to weigh down on my First World generation. It was a seeping, invisible pressure that percolated everything my friends and I heard, saw, touched and breathed. A screaming silence trickling inside our ears.

once upon a house

down payment

I don't remember when we grew so big, but home quickly became too small for young Singaporeans like me, who had everything we wanted and desired what we weren't even sure was out there. Statistics showed that satisfaction with life at home decreased from 62 percent in 1996, to 56 percent in 2000. In 2001, the number of Singaporeans who gave up their citizenship doubled, and by the end of 2003, the net migration rate of Singapore ranked sixth in the world.

In school, my classmates and I were often told that we were the future leaders of Singapore. This would set off a domino bout of eye-rolling among us; but then, no one readily admitted to scoring below 1450 on the SATs either.

The majority of us were breezily fluent in three forms of English. The first, known as Singlish, is our local-speak. It is a mishmash of intonations and hotchpotch grammar stemming from our multi-cultural heritage. The second, the "proper" kind, was what our British teachers shoved down our throats. The third form of English was what we used to converse with each other. This colloquial third was a little confused; it was undecidedly American/British/Singlish all at the same time and was casually interspersed with words like cool/bloody/sian.

Already, we had become self-evolved shape-shifters, assimilators, and migrants. In search of some greener lawn, the same forces that drew our forefathers from all over South East Asia to Singapore in the 1920s now began to pull us away from home.

After completing the Cambridge "A" Level Examination, I applied to Georgetown University and was accepted for the 2001 Fall semester. When I told my parents the news over dinner, my father kept silent. I believe he was mentally calculating how far back I had set his retirement plan. My mother, on the other hand, plunged a porcelain spoon into her watercress soup and argued, "But all your cousins went for college in the U.K.; it's closer to Singapore. Why must you go to the U.S.?"

She paused to regroup.

"And why didn't you apply to Harvard or Princeton? If you got into those schools, or even Yale, it would be a totally different matter. I would tell you

quarter passed

right here at this table, Go!"

I knew my mother was kidding herself. There was no university on this planet so outstanding that it justified my being away from the both of them.

I remember liking the way it sounded in my college acceptance letter, the word "Fall." In Singapore, we had 365 days of blistering heat every year and I associated the cold with wonderful things like glitter-doused puffs of cotton wool pegged to plastic trees during Christmas and family ski trips. Of course, four bitter winters in America changed my mind about climate forever.

When I left for college orientation in August, my first solo stopover flight from Singapore to New York involved equal parts bawling and celebration at the departure gate. I did most of the celebrating while my parents did most of the bawling, though I suspect we exchanged roles soon after I got on the plane.

My mother - whose favorite counter-question for me whenever I asked her to buy me something when I was younger was, "Do you think your father is printing money?" - wrapped her small arms around my neck. Before she pulled away she whispered in my ear, "Don't ever worry about the money, okay? If you are not happy there, just come back. Dawn, when you think you are done, promise me you'll come back to us."

Shiying left for the U.S. a week later.

moving in

"Does your country really cane people?"

"Is chewing gum banned?"

"Aren't you part of China? When are you going to be handed back to them?"

"Is there a standing box you have to book in advance to exercise free speech?"

"How is it that your English is so good?"

"Oh. You've some weird local English over there, right? Say something using it!"

Yes.

Yes.

once upon a house

No. Never.
It's not exactly a box. It's more like a speaker's corner, but yes.
English is our first language.
You wouldn't understand if I spoke it anyway.

During first encounters, I spent a good amount of time responding to commonly-posed inquiries from curious Americans. I used to feel like the Singaporean ambassador in my freshmen dorm. After a while, I took a certain amount of pride in my role, dispelling other myths such as, "All you people are fucking good at Math and shit," and statements like, "Chinese food is awesome. Do Moo Shoo Pork and General Tso's Chicken taste the same in Singapore?" I hadn't heard of these dishes in Asia and honestly never tasted anything quite as bad.

By luck, I had picked a college that was populated by only four other Singaporeans when I arrived. Forming a national-ethnic clique of our own was a pathetic idea. This notion was further deflated by our few failed attempts to meet for dinner.

Social aggregation, studies reveal, is an innate primitive function among animals in a foreign environment. This function establishes a temporary home-away-from-home, because most animals don't fancy change. They like their lives the way they are, and it is mainly humans who exhibit a voracious appetite for disrupting monotony while still craving some form of "sameness" within this change.

On most days across campus, this type of social clotting can be observed in the sporadic clusters of Asians, African Americans, and wealthy, chain-smoking Euros who drift through the predominant sea of white, preppy students. However, because I had no cluster of my own, I was forced - as I had wished for before I came - to acquire my own collection of all-American friends and to suck no less than $200,000 (the cost of tuition) worth of marrow right out of this Red, White, and Blue college experience.

Fitting in didn't turn out to be too hard because being a Chinese girl in America isn't difficult. It didn't matter that I was not "Chinese" but "Singaporean-Chinese" here. Indians, Chinese, Filipinos, Koreans and Japanese are all lumped under the broad category, "Asian." And though America's Asian fetish doesn't quite extend to my Chinese brothers – kudos to whatever pre-conceived notions Hollywood gave them – it placed girls like me at the top of the college social ladder. Because I was not American-born Chinese, I was, like Zhang Ziyi, the authentic stuff.

I could be bitter and say that I left home only to be colonized by the West again, but it was never that dramatic. A Chinese – or, rather, Singaporean – pragmatism permeated my view. I enjoyed my position in the U.S. and, at times, milked it for what it was worth.

Once or twice, having to take a compulsory class which I didn't care for, I would pay my professor an office visit towards the end of the semester. As I sat behind their paper-stacked desks, I often lowered my head and explained in soft, stunted sentences, "You see, I … I try h…hard to speak up in class. But I … I don't come from here, and back home, we … well, women, we aren't used to having voices."

One old man, who held a PhD in East Asian history and wrote intellectual discourses on the Vietnam War, nearly cried. He gave me an A.

wet paint

The Merriam-Webster Dictionary has six definitions of "home," including: one's place of residence; the social unit formed by a family living together; a place of origin; and a familiar setting.

My mother tells me that when I was five, home was a place I was particularly fond of when things didn't work out the way I wanted them to. I typically articulated such sentiments to her by saying, "This sucks – I want to go home."

Maybe this is because the inside of a home is easy to identify when you are five. Home was where I had my bed, my clothes, my floppy Pink Panther, and my parents. It was my contained world. Within it, I knew exactly how everything looked, moved, smelt, felt, and – to my mother's horror – tasted. I also remember the sounds I heard in our old flat: our neighbor's Bose surround sound system vibrating through the brick walls and the clattering of flustered Filipino maids rushing children off to school at 7 a.m. every morning. It was the music I grew up on – the orchestra of television sets, plates, chopsticks, people, dragged furniture, and gossip.

After leaving Singapore, I called home crying about many things. Topics ranged from crashed hard drives to car accidents, boyfriends and missed flights. But I never once called my parents crying that I missed home or that I wanted to come back. It was the Chinese part of me that had too much pride. I don't think I thought much about home, either, once I arrived in America. But missing home was another thing.

You can miss something without having to think of it and I missed home. I didn't miss it in the way that meant I hated America. Even if I didn't find home in the latter, or disagreed with its politics, ironic ethnocentricity, and excessive consumption, there were many things I admired about America. One being how a canonized formula for success seems less-canonized, and how a wider space for differing opinions to co-exist exists.

I loved that people in America tend to be more passionate and entrepreneurial, and most importantly, how most Americans are actually proud to be American. It made me question why growing up, my friends and I weren't proud to be Singaporean.

Once upon a country in 1819, Singapore was founded as a British trading colony by Stamford Raffles. In search of a better life, migrants from all over China, India, Indonesia, Arabia and the Malay Archipelago flocked to the island, which grew into the busiest port in the region. Only in 1965, did Singapore become independent. Today, the little-island-that-could is arguably the most impressive Asian Tiger. It enjoys a well-oiled free market economy, an immaculately-designed city, and one of the highest levels of GDP per capita in the world.

All Singaporeans know this story by heart. We also know that our country owns no natural resources other than a highly educated workforce, and that it was sheer hard work which placed us on the map.

Since my classmates and I were considered "bright," we were expected to condition ourselves to be smarter, faster and better than everyone else in order for our country to survive. Unfortunately, when you spend all your time trying to be "better" than the people around you, it's easy to grow arrogant and feel like

quarter passed

you're too good for those you have bested. I believe this was the problem with kids who grew up the way I did.

Forty years of independence and national history is a blip when plotted against the timelines of countries in Europe or even America. Singapore had no Hellenic Age, Dark Age, no Enlightenment, nor a French Revolution. While the West has already formed a conscious identification with a common civilization, Singapore remains a drifting island with a story that is incomplete.

In the early 1990s, when multinational corporations flooded Singapore, the country was in a race to catch-up with the West. We eagerly cut-and-pasted everything from them: technology, equipment, strategies, policies, attitudes and beliefs. When we surveyed our creation, home looked picture-perfect. Few of us really had time to sit down and think about how, beneath the drying paint, most of us as a nation, felt a little lost.

the square with a triangle hat

Over the past several years, I've spent a substantial amount of time on airplanes. Being away from home has developed a wanderlust within me that lures me away from America and Singapore every chance I get. But most of the time, I am on that same plane flying from East to West and back again.

What I enjoy most is looking out of the oval plastic window just after the plane takes off or before it lands. It is nice to see cities from a distance: cars shriveled to crawling color pixels, houses reduced to monopoly board markers, and roads spanning outwards to form an endless-checkered grid.

When the plane dips, a synthetic voice seeps through the muffled-speakers. It bleeps, "Good afternoon, passengers," and announces the aircraft's arrival at my final destination. I cringe and click the seat buckle shut. I don't have a final destination, and sometimes it bugs me that I may never find one. Singapore is no longer what it used to be for me. Neither is America.

I think when you are so far away from home you often remember things about it that aren't there anymore when you get back - a particular person, the peeling skin of an old building, the smell and weight of the air just before it pours.

once upon a house

Some of these things were never there to start with. But you invented them, so you remember things all the same.

On the other hand, you develop selective amnesia. You forget the things you hated about home, the things you couldn't stand. But the more you miss home, the more it disappears, and the more it disappears, the more you miss what isn't there.

Soon, home becomes this square with a triangle hat, or a long vertical rectangle with 500 tiny squares.

◆◆◆

dawn ng. (24, singapore, singapore)

quarter passed

no ride. by sara sky schutte. (27, milan, italy)

limbo

by morenike balogun

I want the future now, even if days
can no longer be tasted.
To see the ripened fruits of labors
not yet conceived.
Feel the lips of love to be revealed.

My heart beats for it, faster than time
in rhythms that rhyme of opportunities
lost in weeks of simply finding the way.
Doors opened for a million, or merely a dime.

Sweat has poured from it, tears fallen
towards the end of something sweet.
Which suddenly tastes like empty space
filled with uncomfortable comfortables
and almost invisible beauties.

Take me to a second wind, where it all fits.
North, South, East, or West?
'Til my soles bleed for it.
'Til the earth calls for it.
I will run and make the way my own.

morenike balogun.   (25, kobenhavn s, denmark)

quarter passed

stripped corridor. by abdel munem amin. (24, montreal, quebec, canada)

insomnia
by petra kristine turner

eyes closed,
heart pounding,
temples throbbing,
tossing,
dreaming - awake.
i tumble down
to my open window;
look out at the night sky -
the stars, flashing.
i drift out among them,
a dying light,
straining to be seen,
struggling to breathe,
buried by this fog,
this sickening sensation,
this myopic vision -
i can't see;
i can't think;
i can't sleep.
succumbing
to these odd days,
i've slipped
into my past,
into that girl,
into what I left behind:
sorrowful, saddened,

quarter passed

scarred,
misplaced,
dispersed,
so confused,
so tired of sleeping
and dying for something else,
for something real.

◆◆◆

petra kristine turner. (26, edmonton, alberta, canada)

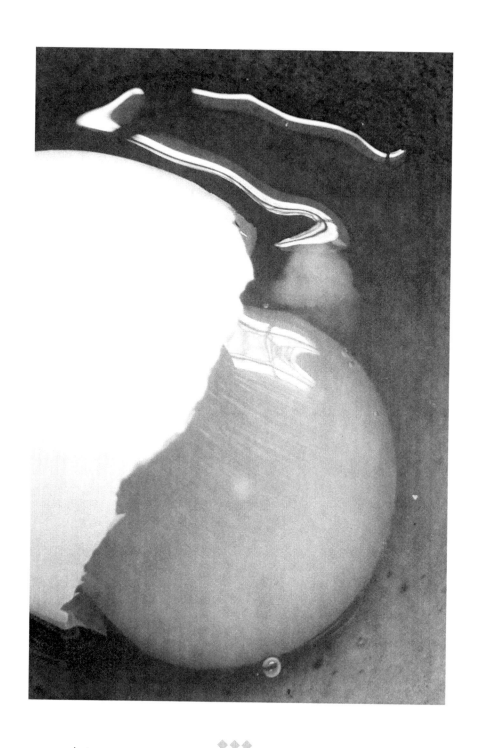

egg chalaza. by clarissa caldwell. (23, boulder, colorado, usa)

quarter passed

the goo inside
by clarissa caldwell

PARTS OF THE EGG: white, yolk, chalaza, germinal disk, shell.

WHITE: Fluid and translucent. A legless jellyfish, a protective amoeba. A mucus bubble shielding fragile contents.
wants: Softness. Opaque light obscures sharp edges.

    I find the green house in August. It is quaint, cozy, just right. Inside, pale gold walls border big windows and splash sunshine across the hardwood floor.
    "This will be my place in Colorado," I think. My first home after college. My little nook in the Rockies. My roommates, friendly strangers, fill the fridge with food labeled ORGANIC and offer me tofu for breakfast.
    Life begins à la Bohemian: no career plan, no health plan, no life-partner, no worries. I sing Spanish to preschoolers and teach them to say, "caballo." I have only one real concern: the inflow of crinkly paper sustenance. The grocery fund, the electricity, the trash bill are all supported by part-time teaching wages and weekend tip money, earned foaming milk for pricey lattes in a corner coffee shop.
    I am young, I tell myself.
    I am happy-ish, even – except for the occasional swell of poetic loneliness, burning my throat like a ribbon of dry air. I wash it down with a glass of wine, insisting on remaining romantic. Myopic. Counting pennies and flittering from moment to moment.

YOLK: Plump and yellow like a southwestern sunshine. Safe and fluid, a body of change, a potential fetus of goo that needs nurturing to grow.

the goo inside

wants: Warmth. Eggs need warmth to make shapes from inconsequential blobs.

Winter suddenly descends, transforming the houses and trees with a frosty white mask. Temperatures plummet and tears crystallize on my cheeks when I walk outside.

"We are poor," my roommate says.

"Yes, we are," I agree.

In late November, we turn the thermostat to 50°, just enough to prevent the pipes from bursting. We put plastic on the windows to ward off the wintry winds whistling through thin panes. Viewing the world through sheets of wrinkled Saran Wrap I wonder why I'd moved into the freezing, vomit-green place with yellow pee-colored walls. Cold, ugly, cold, ugly place.

My fingers turn perpetually gray, like the sky outside, stiff and useless. Some time in December I stop drawing, stop playing guitar, stop daydreaming. I eat oatmeal and sleep in the fetal position.

Surviving is doable, though dreary and dismal. Day-by-day has become paycheck-to-paycheck. What if my desires, my delight, my destiny all freeze in the frigid air? What if my potential dries out like the crusty skin on my neglected kneecaps?

I see my life: working like a slave, living hand-to-mouth, constantly cold, a stone in frozen mud.

CHALAZA: Resembling a fragment of white floss; prevents yolk from moving around and bashing against shell walls. A security rope; sanity, family, fallback.

wants: Protection. A mother hen can flash light across the shadows.

My mom gives me her old space heater at Thanksgiving.

"One day you'll realize…," she says again, "One day you'll realize this is just your life. Just your life, and you're living it."

Imagine saying to a child, "One day you'll realize, this is just candy. Just your candy, and you're eating it." Just candy? The child thinks, "But, it's jellybeans and gummy bears! Hershey's kisses and Snickers bars!"

quarter passed

Mom repeats, despite my objections, "It's just your life."

On my worst days, "It's just your hormones. All through your twenties," she coos soothingly, "the hormones go up and down."

"Down," I mumble, loathing myself for worrying my dear mother.

She sighs. And she tells me, again, her mantra, "Go have some tea and take a hot bath."

"Okay," I say. "I love you." I hang up the phone and, as I always do after a Mom conversation, heat the stove for some chamomile tea. I would never use our bathtub. In fact, one day we extract a rat-size clump of hair from the drain.

"It's a dreadlock," a roommate muses.

"It was probably Maria's," the other agrees with a nod.

My bathtub is refuge to tangled hair; my house is ice cold; my life is lonely; my body is tired; my mind is pathetic, inconsistent. And my Mom is right. Right about hormones and life, right about hot baths, right about my "First World problems" and first class folly. Fine. And my serenity still comes and goes like a drunk monkey on a floating trampoline.

GERMINAL DISK: Tiny red dot that only vegetarians notice, like a broken blood vessel on a baby's face. A mark of fear: becoming another miniscule speck in the world, rolling along, unnoticed, down someone's throat and into the abyss of intestines.
wants: A nesting spot - a place where it's appreciated.

"I'm going to move in with my parents," I sigh into the telephone, "unless a miracle job appears on the horizon - any horizon."

"No shame in moving home," my friend responds. "No shame at all nowadays. We're like boomerangs."

"Yeah," I agree. "Maybe it is because we're getting married later, and we need taking care of. Social animals, we humans. Love, love, love…"

Several months ago, I quit my two dead-end jobs, and began another dead-end job as a personal assistant. I spend my days returning someone else's unwanted merchandise, buying different kinds of cereal and picking up deer poop scattered

the goo inside

across the lawn.

The sweet, pregnant lady I work for has the ideal American life: a happy marriage, happy home. Sometimes I consider moving to another country to avoid taxes and broken picket fences. Do I just want to be somebody, somewhere? I am unique. Just like everybody else.

"Maybe we should go to Bulzinania together," I say to a friend.

"Yes," she chirps. "Who will buy the camel when we get there?"

SHELL: Pale ceramic-like surface. Looks deceptively strong and protective, breaks under pressure.
wants: Transformation. No warmth, no mother hen, no place.

"I know you're right. I won't starve," I say to my sister, tears licking the rims of my eyes.

Beneath the weight of my fears, the infinite expectations, the solitude, I am sinking, sinking into the sorrow like a leaf into wet mud. This terror-filled melancholic swirl is rife with inventive absurdity. I flush down like a toilet, until those hormones turn the juke box on again, and I'm okay, laughing at the teenage angst, and flexing my muscles to dance around the next emotional brouhaha, carefree and rolling.

Why do I bother with the shell? The inside spills out eventually - promising, but tender, like a blossom in early spring.

Goodbye, egg. Now I can send this little blurb into the world, hoping someone will catch it and hatch somehow, blinking open their eyes to see a phosphorescent land of bulbous yolks and bright germinal disks.

❖❖❖

clarissa caldwell. (23, boulder, colorado, usa)

quarter passed

untitled. by jonathan thomas. (28, hendersonville, tennessee, usa)

fuel

by stephan delbos

It is not a fear of darkness,
But of the things we may not see
At dawn.

It is not a fear of silence,
But of the words we may not hear
Again.

It is not a fear of solitude,
But of a separated unity
That has not ever been.

It is not a fear of dying,
But of unbecoming
Anything.

◆◆◆

stephan delbos. (23, prague, czech republic)

quarter passed

herbergi. by ólöf jóhannsdóttir. (25, reykjavík, iceland)

mother

by bridgette holmes

there is a place
where we cannot see the road
through our tears
and we are constantly looking for answers

this place
a blank spot in our minds
our plan not quite ironed out
instead: wet, soiled and wrinkled

we have walked with one another many times
we hold hands but our grasp is not tight
I often wonder if this connection will be lost
after we move around the next bend

perspective changes, as age sets in –
after seeing mother through two divorces
alone, sixty-two or three
a dog, a cigarette and a can of beer as company
on cold winter nights
worrying about the next tax bill
and the man down the street who gives her money

I wonder, can I be her?
if I am careless in my life decisions
jump in too excitedly into the pool of commitment

quarter passed

will my daughter be as unforgiving as I?

Every ounce of me loathes the idea
of ending up like that
yet, the more I work not to be her,
the more I need her
I need her to see my success,
brag about my adventures,
see that I am something she can be proud of

I am an egoist,
a hypocrite
and a coward in the same breath

because I cannot admit what she gave to me
I am too shortsighted to notice
the virtues that allowed me to grow,
to get here,
to think,
to know
both what I want
and what I will never want

◆◆◆

bridgette holmes. (26, saratoga springs, new york, usa)

fire and ice. by elvina trixie. (21, shanghai, china)

quarter passed

confession
by rhiannon elston

One day I woke up in a bathroom stall.

There was blood caked on my arm, in splodges. It had dripped there from some higher level. My head, maybe. It damn well hurt enough.

I unfolded myself from the floor, shuddering as I pried my hands from the sticky unknown substance that gripped at my skin, reluctant to let me go. Outside, I could hear the party raging. Inside, I was cold, and alone.

The blood traced back to my nose, leading down my face in a thin, wormy track. With my silver party dress twisted like a rope around my body, I felt so far from the glamour queen I'd been when the night began. We'd sauntered into the club like rock stars, me and my mates. Straight to the bar for a double and a chaser. Where were those mates now? I couldn't even remember who I'd come with.

I clambered to my feet and felt the repercussions pounding in my head. A dull, rhythmic bass pounded, echoing the distant music wafting in from somewhere beyond the stall.

"How the hell," my thoughts hammered in time with the beat, "did you get yourself into this situation?" At what point did having fun turn into this?

Dry tears choked my eyes and I mashed at them with grimy hands. When the wracking sobs were gone I pulled out my phone. The blank screen stared back at me. No messages. Not one. What to do next?

For a moment, everything stopped. A silent conversation between two heartbeats. Pride, I realized, no longer mattered. My hands seemed to work of their own accord, bringing the handset to my face.

"Mum," I sighed when the ringing at the other end stopped, "I need you."

rhiannon elston. (25, waverton, australia)

fuck

by meaghan e. doss

So sick of
climbing through my passenger's side
missing my door handle
city boys looking right through me
not keeping my passwords straight
the cable bill and
its evil twin the electric
friends with tracked arms
cold, cold, cold, and snow
sleeping diagonally on my bed so I'm not so lonely
loans and loans and still no money
my three jobs
and not a single fucking pair
of knitted mittens.

meaghan e. doss. (20, new paltz, new york, usa)

quarter passed

29

by dylan mark belden

Life – up to this point – has been full of opportunities, yes, but mostly opportunities lost. I know, I know, all the things that have happened so far add up to who I am now, and I've learned lessons, blah, blah, blah, but it still feels like a lot of time has passed and not much substance has come of it.

The past twenty-nine years have been a dress rehearsal for real life. Or even a non-dress rehearsal; one of those rehearsals that's so raw and not ready to be seen by critics that the actors don't even bother getting into costume. They're all standing around in jeans and t-shirts. Tennis shoes, too. They're blocking their movements. That's what my life to-date has been like – going through the motions.

Growing up? Yeah, sure. Did that. Tried Cub Scouts for a while. Tried karate for a few weeks. Played the clarinet for a month in fourth grade. Played T-ball; played baseball. Camped out in right or left field, looking for four-leaf clovers in the grass, swatting at gnats, maybe looking up when a bat hit the ball. Went on trips. The Badlands, Montana, the Apple River. Played video games in the basement. Played Monopoly with the family (which always ended with my mom yelling at my brother for cheating and my brother storming off and my mom vowing that we'd never play that goddamn game again). Listened to baseball on the radio. Watched *The Simpsons*. Built traps for squirrels with buckets held up by sticks.

Did college. Slept in a loft. Drank Mountain Dew and cheap beer out of a tiny fridge. Learned a thing or two; got excited (or at least a little worked up) about a couple of new ideas. Figured out how to take a city bus. Wore dirty clothes because I didn't have enough coins to wash them in the dorm basement. Waited with anticipation for that biweekly $50 check from working at the cafeteria. Walked back and forth across the "quad," sometimes wondering why it was called that, and who decided to call it that, and where exactly its boundaries were? Keggers? Frat parties? Pep rallies? Protest rallies? Hanging out at campus bars with the liberal professors? Nerd uprisings? Bah. Apparently those things only happen in movies.

Finished college. What now? Got married. Got a job. Had a son. Changed jobs. Got a couple of cats. Changed jobs again. Broke up with the wife. Kept the son, though. He's good. He gets to stay.

Through it all, what has driven me? Not some sense of purpose. Not the pursuit of a goal. It has been more like I'm trying to look busy, because somebody might be watching. It has felt like it didn't really matter what I did, as long as it wasn't something dangerous or tacky, like getting hooked on meth and stealing copper wire from construction sites so I could sell it at recycling centers. As long as I appeared to be productive, seemed to be pursuing the same things other people pursue, I met the status quo.

Did I want to attend that particular university? Did I want to go into the profession I chose? Did I want to get married? It seemed like I did at the time. Sort of. But, looking back, it all seems like it was a show; a One Act play. What I thought I was supposed to do. Not the real thing. Not what I really wanted. I don't feel like I truly chose any of it.

Twenty-nine years after I entered the world, naked and slimy and annoyed, I'm still waiting for life to really start. And I'm still kind of annoyed.

I wonder if young adults of past generations had it easier. The formula was easy; it was laid right out for you, and you had a frowning alliance of mothers and aunts, pastors and neighbors, ready to push you along the path: Get a good job. Get married. Have a family. Complain about the in-laws. Uphold family values. Go to Disneyland a few times. The daughter plays with dolls; the son wants a BB gun. And so forth. Was it ever really like that? Probably not.

But it wasn't like this before, either. Expectations have either disappeared entirely or broadened to the point where they might as well not exist anymore. What's left is freedom (terrible, terrible freedom!), but without guidance about what to do with it.

The mothers and aunts these days try to meddle sometimes, but I think it's kind of half-hearted, and in my case it seems like they have their own things to worry about, anyway. The pastors are still somewhere out there, but their audi-

quarter passed

ences are shrinking, especially when you consider the under-thirty crowd. When the young ones do show up, the pastors wouldn't dare condemn their choices, or they might not come back! The neighbors don't seem to care anymore, as far as I can tell. I assume they're there, but I've never gossiped with one over a picket fence.

People like me, these days, we have to figure everything out for ourselves. But it's not that easy. The first step is figuring out that we have to figure it out, see? Then we can actually begin to figure it out. Some people never even get to that point.

But in the past year, I've had an awakening. I've realized that going limp and letting the wind blow you wherever it goes is no way to be. Somebody's got to take charge of this life and it might as well be me, since it is mine, after all.

It's not uncommon anymore for the twenties to be an extended adolescence, full of experimentation. Maybe six years in college, or maybe a couple of job changes after college (or maybe no college at all), or maybe a few years of a soul-sucking job and then college as a way out. Without the pressure for us twentysomethings to couple up and settle down, we can do that.

In my case, there was a different kind of experimentation. A false start of sorts. Quick marriage, quick transition into a career that I've stuck with for eight years, the appearance of heading down that more traditional path; that stable, reliable path that's such a cliché precisely because it's been a cultural standard for a long time. But now, a crossroads. Call it a quarter-life crisis if you must or blame it on the Saturn Return if you're into that kind of thing, but it's happening.

Time to stop doing what seems easy at the time, or what I think others probably expect me to do. Time to figure out what I can do that will actually make me happy and maybe actually accomplish something positive in this mad, mad, mad, mad, kooky, crazy world. There's a misconception that the under-thirty crowd is full of slackers. Sure, a few of us are slackers. Video games, for instance, have an alarming degree of staying power among young men of my generation. But, for the most part, I think people want to do something memorable, to be someone, to make a difference. Some of us just aren't sure how to do it. In the absence of rigid cultural standards that make choices easy, what did you expect to happen?

But waking up and answering the question is the first step, and those of us who take that step set ourselves up for life's Act Two with plenty of hope and possibilities. Hell, people live 'til they're like eighty these days; we've got plenty of time left. We can afford to piss away the twenties, as long as it serves some purpose, moves us along a path toward some greater awareness or understanding. That's what it seems to have done for me. I'll be thirty in just a few months and I'm looking at that nice, round number not as an end to youth, but as a new beginning.

◆◆◆

dylan mark belden.   (29, st. paul, minnesota, usa)

quarter passed

kids. by vishal shah. (29, london, england)

2

tradition

religious conflict. by aaron alper. (24, st. petersburg, florida, usa)

keeping the faith

by ruthie kott

"Eat me, Ruthie... You know that you want me. I'm tasty and nutritious. You didn't even keep kosher for Passover last year, why start now?" The unopened box of whole wheat spaghetti in my cabinet is relentless beside the pretzels, jelly beans, and lemon-pepper-flavored couscous peeking out at me. A box of Manischewitz unsalted matzah on the kitchen table promptly chimes in:

"Ruthie, I'm disappointed in you. Even though I cause constipation and am exceptionally bland, I was the only food that your people ate while trekking through the desert after escaping from slavery. And you can't even spare your precious pasta for seven measly nights."

My eyes wander slowly back to the spaghetti. I could drizzle my deliciously decadent homemade peanut butter/honey/soy sauce concoction over the pasta, and then garnish it with fried tofu and sautéed orange peppers. Or, I could eat peanut butter and honey on matzah. It's the third night, and I'm quickly running out of innovative ways to fill-in-the-blank in "[blank] on matzah." I'm alone in the apartment; nobody's watching me but God. But even God takes a break sometimes, right? He won't notice if I sneak in a little pasta.

I missed the sedar at the Jewish Center on the first night of Passover. I'm familiar with the Jewish Center but we haven't exactly been on good terms. I've spent precious time seated around the large rectangular table in the middle of the fluorescent-lit main room through two semesters of college: Multi-Ethnic Israel (B-) and the Hebrew Bible (C+).

Earlier this year on Rosh Hashanah, I ventured through those two glass doors for the first time in two and a half years. That morning, my Jewish Studies minor roommate, Rachel Levine, knocked on my door and asked in her innocent voice,

keeping the faith

"Ruthie, are you coming to services?" with narrowed, judging eyes.

I hesitated. Rosh Hashanah is one of the most important and holy holidays in Judaism but the "Baruch atah's" and the "Kaddishes" in these services mean nothing more to me than the poetic babble of a childhood nursery rhyme, a kind of reverse "Ring around the Rosy." ('Please rise' rather than 'and we all fall down.') Though I wasn't looking directly into Rachel's eyes for fear of turning to stone, her prying gaze pushed harder.

A few days earlier, one of my Gentile roommates, Lauren, had commented on how the few times she'd been to the Jewish Center with Rachel for Shabbat services or bagel brunches, she'd felt like no one really wanted her there. Rachel shook her head dramatically, scrunching up her nose and squinting her eyes.

"No, Lauren, the Rabbi loves it when non-Jews come to the Center. I think the people they get suspicious of are the Jews who aren't really involved." She un-squints and looks directly at me.

So, on that Rosh Hashanah morning, after what felt like ten minutes, I looked up at Rachel and stuttered, "Um, sure, I'll go to services."

I made us late. Sprinting through the glass doors that open into the Jewish Center, we snagged the first available seats we saw and sat down with our prayer books. Wanting to avoid a scene, I turned to the yarmulke-sporting sophomore next to me, sneaking a peek over his shoulder.

"Page 142," I whispered to Rachel.

She nodded quietly and flipped conscientiously to page 142. Chest still heaving, I sat back in my chair and listened to the Rabbi chant the words that I'd heard so many times before. Suddenly, in the middle of the "Sh'ma," the most important prayer of the service, the loud twang of Stevie Wonder's "Superstition" rang through the air.

I looked down at the purse lying at my feet and spotted specks of neon blue light glowing through the small gaps of the zipper. My face burned. Everyone's heads flipped around to identify the heathen whose cell phone was ringing in the middle of High Holiday services. Rachel's head swiveled so quickly that I could actually hear the "whoosh" of her neck as I groped desperately for the "off" button. It's not a movie theater; I shouldn't need animated buckets of popcorn to

quarter passed

remind me, "Shhhhh! No talking in the House of God! And please make sure your cell phones are OFF."

Despite my Jewish New Year's humiliation, I planned for weeks to attend the sedar on the first night of Passover. I kept the yellow sign-up form with the tear-off bottom in my bag for weeks, filled out and ready to hand in to the office in the basement of the Chapel. Somehow, I just never got around to that part. The week before Passover, I got an e-mail: "There are still open spots! Just show up, bring $10 and join us for Passover sedar!"

On the day of, however, my looming thesis deadline overpowered my craving for hardboiled eggs and horseradish. Non-Jewish Lauren went with Rachel to commemorate our freedom from slavery in Egypt while I stayed locked up, writing in my room.

I had vowed to try really, really hard to stay kosher for Passover this year. Last year at this time, I was living abroad in Sydney, Australia where kosher wasn't exactly on the menu, and I felt extremely guilty. My roommates in Australia were two girls from Louisiana who had never seen a Jew in their lives.

On the first night of Passover Down Under, while I was guiltily joking about my "bad Judaism," my roommates were attending a sedar at the flat of their new Jewish friend, Susi Green. They came back that night after the sedar, cheeks red and glowing with Passover wine and stomachs full of matzah ball soup and charoset.

"Ruthie," they chanted, "we're better Jews than you are!"

I have never fasted on Yom Kippur. I eat shrimp and bacon. I can't answer my little brother when he asks why he should believe in God. I have a tattoo. My nose is small. My cell phone goes off in the middle of Rosh Hashanah services. My Catholic roommate attends sedars while I sit at home. I've never dated a Jewish guy. Except for the fact that I was forced to attend Hebrew School for eleven years and that I am severely affected by Jewish guilt, what about me is Jewish?

The pasta and the matzah lie side-by-side on the counter. I look from one to the other for five minutes before I bend over to grab a pot from the cabinet below the sink. Filling the pot up with water, I start the burner on the stove and put it on to boil. Matzah just isn't going to cut it anymore. As the water boils

keeping the faith

and I'm breaking the pasta in half to add to the steaming pot, I hear the front door slam and I freeze. I whip around to find Rachel waltzing into the kitchen. She zeroes in like a laser beam on the box of spaghetti, the absence of a kosher "K" blaring like the neon blue ringing cell phone. Her eyes narrow.

"I just want some chocolate so badly," she whines, those glaring eyes moving from the pasta to my reddening face. "But, you know, it's Passover and I just can't bring myself to cheat."

ruthie kott. (22, brighton, massachusetts, usa)

quarter passed

untitled. by ksenia shashounova. (24, st. petersburg, russia)

traveling riverside blues

by lucy boydon

It was always that bridge, always at the back of my mind, where I walk to escape or stay grounded.

A little history please, Miss? This bridge, this 'always' bridge, resides in my hometown of Edinburgh. Strictly speaking, I suppose, it's on the outside - straddling the Firth of Forth going over to the west (spit) of Scotland. There are a lot of stupid politics in Scotland that most people don't understand, but this is the same as in any country or city. I'm sure there are always wee factions and niggles over who lives where and which place is worse, for some antiquated reason that no one really remembers. In Scotland it's the east/west thing - hardly ganglands - but basically, they think that we're the 'English' side of Scotland, and we think that Glaswegians erroneously think that they're the 'real capital'.

Don't get me wrong, I don't live by these borders - I have friends that are from the 'other side'. And in a country whose entire population is the size of London (or maybe even less), you've got to wonder why we even bother. It's a silly joke, really, a drunken argument that's always executed in the same way but never resolved, and that's immediately forgotten but forever there. Like y-fronts and taper-leg trousers, it's never going to go away, annoying, unnecessary and unashamedly silly.

Now, back to the bridge. It's called the Forth Railway Bridge (score one for the 'originality of ye olde Scottish architects') and it's made of iron. The only way you get a decent view of it, instead of being blindingly skewed by the sun, is to stand parallel to it on the Forth Road Bridge (score two for the originality of said architects), which allows pedestrians and cars to cross. In tourist shops they sell pictures of it, spiky and wavy, pretty looking, inevitably

quarter passed

set against a beautiful blue sky and slashing sun; the small villages to the left looking quaint and 'inherently Scottish'. In reality, this bridge is never free of fuming buzzing trains, the weather is never so blue and there is an ugly hotel that dominates the landscape (all carefully photoshopped out). The ploy works. Tourists buy these pictures as 'a bit of Scotland' they can lug home, but this airbrushed version is not the bridge I like.

My mother, in one of her more optimistic phases, once decided that making my sister and me walk along the Road Bridge would be fun: a mile of smog on a blazing hot day with the sea scorching your eyes, wicked winds making the bridge sway, and ugly hotel wankers and their mistresses being the only thing we moved towards with plastic pink sandals scratching tiny feet. Still, she was absolutely right.

I remember years later, watching some ancient video about the Tacoma Narrows Bridge and how it warped and jumped just before collapsing. It reminded me of that day. To me, walking on a quarter-mile high bridge wasn't at all scary, even when the wind whipped up my little blue dress and yanked the red ribbon out of my white hair. It was a tool to stare at the other, more interesting orange Railway Bridge.

I was only about seven at the time and was still completely unaware that I could be hurt by anything other than my brother's fists, my sister's nails, and gravel hitting my knees when I'd been running. When you're little, you're always running, despite the fact that you have all the time in the world, and being late is never going to have serious consequences, and the person chasing you is never going to do you any serious harm. It's all fun and games until the running for running's sake takes on a whole new meaning. I should lose a few pounds. I'm going to miss that bus. Someone's following me. It suddenly becomes something to be wary of. It means a nuisance at best and has a serious edge of danger to it at worst.

So, I hung over the edge in between sprints and looked at the blue, blue water under my bridge, knowing it killed my mother every time I did it. When I was young, I was never wary of heights. I was first to the top of the Eiffel Tower on a school trip, pressing my nose against the glass; I was seduced by heights and the idea of floating weightlessly down, not screaming but drifting listlessly – it wasn't ever the landing I anticipated, it was just the idea of falling like that dream I've had hundreds of times.

For as long as I can remember, my mother has always been absolutely terrified of heights, and I never really understood why as a child. Now I'm scared too. It's an irrational fear, like any phobia. It's probably the result of my youthful imagination. I would see myself falling, but I was immortal then and it was beautiful, guided and gentle. Now I feel it like my mother, acid in my stomach and sweat on my forehead - I could die at any second if someone pushed me or if I lost my footing or if I had sweaty hands on a railing, or for any number of reasons that are highly unlikely. But it's honestly not that bad. And I suppose sometimes one needs to remember how easily one can die.

The most fascinating thing about the Railway Bridge was always the men who worked on it. No Edwardian architect had an inkling of any possible fault in the flawless plan of using iron almost exclusively in the building of a bridge above sea water. The great thing about being dead is that no one can argue with you about anything, and if anyone tries to pin anything on you, it won't get very far because there will always be those people who want to protect the family or the tradition - or both. However, being dead doesn't make you any less responsible for your missteps or oversights.

Naughty bridge. So naughty that thousands of men have had to give up most of their lives to painting anti-rusting agent on the bloody thing. When they finish one small section, they start the next, suspended thousands of yards up by little pulleys that looked about as safe as a raw, year-old egg. And when they finish all the sections, they start the whole thing again.

When I was seven, I thought this was the best job in the world, this living above water in boundless weightlessness. It was my ideal job as it combined two of my favourite things: painting and danger. What could be more fun?! Paint, paint, paint, then it's time for your milk break. Paint, paint, paint, until the end of time or the end of the bridge - whichever came first. My bet was on the bridge. I looked over at the flaky, rusty bridge, hanging half over the side in my anxiousness, not holding and not caring, smelling the salty sea and wanting to throw my shoe in the water to make that satisfying splashy noise. Clearly I

quarter passed

was kidding myself; there was no way I could tell the bright yellow blobs apart. Paint, paint, paint.

I often wonder how they do it without going mad. There's monotony, and then there's spending your days doing something that you know will never be complete, a great, big, huge circle of a job, of which no one will ever find the beginning, nor the end. Still, there's always comfort to be had from knowing where to go at what time and knowing what you're doing without having to ask and feel like a numptie. This was the epitome of job security, a lifelong profession on that orange bridge, so beautiful against that backdrop of villages and hills and the blue sky.

lucy brydon. (22, edinburgh, scotland)

untitled. by laila antone habash. (21, ramallah, west bank)

my own woman
by rebecca peacock

I was supposed to be different.
That's what my father tells me,
As he watches me pull a turkey from the oven.
He is sorry for my domesticity.
I can hear it in the tone of his voice,
See it in the cold glance
That he gives me
As I busily baste the over-sized bird.
I know that he is disappointed,
That all my big talk about adventures,
About changing the world, about leaving my mark,
Have come down to this.
He can't see past the apron or the diamond ring,
To the woman that I still am.
In his eyes I have become the anti-feminist,
A disgrace to all those women he so admired
As they stood around burning their bras.
I wonder why
He can't see that I have found a balance.

rebecca peacock. (24, baltimore, maryland, usa)

my ohio
by michelle hensarling

Every night before bed and in the morning, outside - where crows hang low and cry ominously, asking what caused their crooked behavior - the wind is blowing and bellowing, as it always has and always will. The eerie sound seems to float across I-45, along the phone lines row-by-row.

God took my smile and asked me if He could borrow it until Tuesday. I was really going to need it as I remained here alone, standing in line at the grocery store. My dad left me waiting in this place for too long. I pick up these broken pieces put them in my Father's hands, hoping trust will come back again.

Corporations grow where I used to lay my head - in this place up north, this place so fragile and cold, this place I called my own. This place, my Ohio, empty and void, like the endless roads it takes to get there again.

Nobody really has a plan to stand on this street corner broke and undone, trying to hold on to something they never had. Some call it hope. Others, perhaps, faith. But to me, it's the truth, reality, honesty if you will.

Everyone is raising their hands at church today, asking for God to catch them as they fall. Fall far away from anything a preacher says. God is whispering back to me in this place, *Where do we go from here?*

This is my Ohio, full of faith and devoid of opportunity. This is my Ohio, stolen and slaughtered. Oh, this place I loved so long ago. Frozen in a church somewhere beneath all the lies.

I forgot to take the garbage out. Dad finally comes home with a black bag; Mom is in it, burned, scarred, and dead. Dad stole my smile that God rightfully gave back to me. Took me by the hair, up the down staircase, releasing a slight giggle in the air.

His eyes and arms captured me - drug me from this place I whispered to… Dad shakes his head and tells me to be still for a moment so he can burn the house of

quarter passed

my childhood down. Later to be boarded up by government men.

Phone lines reach my grip and I dial three numbers that represent so much more now. But I am empty of words, not a sound in my mind.

Firemen ask me to let go of the window. Sparrows and crows fly above me, as the wind bellows and belches, caressing the fire to grow.

God misses my smile and tries to steal it off my father's face as police come by with red and blue lights, like those popsicles I used to eat when it was hot.

As phone lines start to disappear, the interstate highway shies away as well. The grass has taken back what rightfully belonged to it for so many years. That was my Ohio, speeding away from me in the thick rearview mirror of a police car.

Sparrows singing their harmonies, telling me to let go and be free. I am still in line at the grocery store. I am waiting for him to call me. Mom sighs in her indecision - whether to stay or to go - but the next thing I know she is gone. Time floods my memory. Find the places I used to go.

This is my Ohio, swelling under the sun, shackled by streets I once called home, melting like plastic to my mind. Falling so far away, even God could never go-

Back, to my Ohio.

michelle hensarling. (22, houston, texas, usa)

quitting
by dana goldman

Maybe it's a world record? In twenty-three years and ten months, I never quit anything. Not that it was my choice, really. Growing up, my parents brainwashed me with the value of commitment, whether I liked it or not (and I didn't). No matter how mundane the activity, loyalty and dedication came first - as if for every after-school club that I joined, I'd unwittingly signed up for a lifetime membership.

Want to skip a soccer practice? Too bad. Come home early from summer camp, where I spent most of my time sending tear-stained letters home? No way. Stay home from school? I'd need at minimum a 100-degree fever. And if I don't want to practice the cello? No excuses. I knew the refrain by age ten: "You made a commitment."

Just replace the song "Tradition" in "Fiddler on the Roof" with one called "Commitment" and that about sums up my family, minus the shtetl and the cow.

My parents multi-tasked, teaching commitment and indoctrinating guilt at the same time. How would I feel if everyone else quit? How would I ever accomplish anything if I quit? Did I really want to see myself as a quitter?

Just when I began imagining life as a confederate in some dark netherworld of quitters, baby eaters and fascists, my mom would chime in.

"And besides," she would say, "you have no choice."

As I got older the stakes got higher. As a teenager, I had more autonomy over choosing my obligations, but still carried the burden of keeping them. Fortunately, I found that going to college out-of-state was a convenient way to avoid quitting commitments, guilt-free. I didn't quit playing the cello; I left for college. I didn't quit childhood friendships that had obviously been outgrown; I left for college. I didn't quit my job working at a bookstore; I left for college, and could my boss perhaps send my last paycheck to my address there?

quarter passed

The upshot, though, is that up until last year, all I'd ever quit were a few old boyfriends and the consumption of meat (which I'd only quit for a time - a temporary suspension). But the streak couldn't last forever. My post-college dream job, teaching writing, was giving me nightmares in which my boss would order me to write grants and mow lawns. Never mind that I had been in the professional world for all of two years and that the proverbial grind was at a grassroots nonprofit doing good deeds. Despite its ideal nature, I became short with my boyfriend and friends, and soon found myself eating artificially flavored root beer candy - a true sign that something had gone wrong.

I could quantify all my complaints, but acting on them was a different story in a completely unfamiliar genre. My commitment wasn't working for me, but learning how to get out of it would be solely up to me.

After I first acknowledged my unhappiness at work, I spent the next few months panicking and planning in equal proportions. It wasn't so much money that worried me; I had enough saved to keep me going for a month or two. No, what worried me more were the human-relations aspects of resigning. I made Venn diagrams to anticipate my boss's potential reactions and spoke with both a job counselor and a regular counselor, who thankfully did not make me re-hash my history of summer camp homesickness or soccer team ambivalence, or any other childhood tragedy that left scars on my psyche. The breakthrough came when I realized that my fear was not so much about the act of leaving, but the act of disappointing others - in this case, my coworkers and boss.

The office culture had dictated that we weren't employees, but a team. We didn't have meetings; we had check-ins. We didn't have individual offices; we were told we were nonhierarchical, and so shared one divider-free space. I had seen all of my coworkers cry at one point or another. We were told we had been hired because we had convictions and passion. We were told that believing in our work meant willingly sacrificing our vacations and days off and evenings for it. I needed to leave. But, how could I leave something that made me believe I was more than just a worker drone? And now that I was an adult, could I really choose to pack my bags, unlace my cleats, or put down my bow and go home?

I could, but only when the burden of holding in those two magic words, "I

quitting

quit," began pressing down on me more than the weight of my "I do" commitment. Finally, I knew I either needed to say "I quit," or resort to the other magic words for those of us who struggle with anxiety: "I need medication."

And so, last spring, I took the leap. The magic words ended up being a little gentler than I had imagined. "I need to give notice" doesn't have quite the bite of "I quit."

But the Venn diagrams and endless conversations I'd had beforehand helped. My boss was surprisingly supportive, as were my coworkers. And I couldn't have anticipated the immediate sense of relief I felt - even before I actually left. Quitting was the best and cheapest medication of all.

That was almost a year ago, and I'm at a new job now, one I like. I make less money, but I don't need as much either. My anxiety is gone. So is my need for therapists to debrief with and root beer candy to distract me. I am content with my choice, my commitment, and yet, I know that if I needed to, I could quit tomorrow. It wouldn't be pleasant, but I also wouldn't need to agonize or write out a script for what I'd say. I know now the world does not end - or begin - when I leave something or arrive somewhere. It still turns without me in motion.

As a quitter, I hope I can be a role model to my peers and elders who've lived by the same "Fiddler on the Roof" script that I have, and who are ready for that same old soundtrack to end. If I'm describing you, it helps to practice two simple, liberating words: the strong "I", the curt "quit." Say them to yourself now - that's the first step in saying them to anyone else. I quit. I quit. I quit.

dana goldman. (24, atlanta, georgia, usa)

quarter passed

cold feet. by ryan jernigan. (24, lawton, oklahoma, usa)

in those years we lived our best

by bryan david blake

I

It was a cold, windy day, though warm for Norfolk in February, when my friend dropped me off at the air terminal on the Naval Base. I sat in the terminal arranging my travel paperwork and watching the people around me. They were an altogether strange breed of travelers: mustached sailors in stone-washed jeans and 'cruise jackets' sporting military-regulation haircuts shining like beacons against their civilian clothes; Navy wives in sweatpants and house slippers passively attempting to reign in their seven horribly behaved kids; the rarer type acting disinterested and trying not to advertise to the world at large his association with the United States Navy.

Looking around, it dawned on me that this was going to be a long trip, all the more so because I had no idea what awaited me on the other side of the ocean. I wasn't sure if anyone would be waiting for me in Naples; I wasn't even sure if anybody knew I was coming. For now, though, all I could focus on was the fact that this flight was going to consist of screaming infants, oblivious parents, bad food and horrible, Navy-centric conversation.

I was not at all in any state of mind to deal with the situation, so I did my best to bury my nose in The Great Shark Hunt, hoping nobody would try and strike up a conversation. I was going to Naples to get away from this sort of thing, and all I wanted was to hide among the locals and avoid American contact as much as possible. I'd had enough sailor talk and, at any rate, my sea stories were mostly bitter testaments to my miserable 'career' that I really didn't care to discuss. All that concerned me was that I was no longer on sea duty, I'd never again have to get underway, and I was looking at two solid years of shore time before I left this Navy gig behind and hopefully moved on to something more meaningful. I was excited to get to Naples, but the apprehension was growing inside that I had no inkling of what to do once I got there. I planned on sleeping as much as possible now and figuring the rest out later.

We arrived in Naples at around six in the morning, a chilly Italian sunrise coming up over Mount Vesuvius off in the distance. I fumbled around for my orders and passport, grabbed my luggage, and headed outside. At this point, I really had no idea where to go. No one was there to meet me, and there were no visible buses or hotel shuttles. Light rain began coming down as I struggled with my sea duffel and garment bag. I realized that I was in a little over my head. Luckily, a morning commuter stopped and walked with me to the Capo Inn, the transient lodging hotel on the Naval Base. As it turned out, the commuter was a commander in my future building, and he gave me some phone numbers to call after I got settled.

After settling in at the inn, I put on my Service Dress Blue uniform, called my office, and went down to the lobby to wait for someone to meet me. I watched the Italian television in the lobby and got an overwhelming desire to get off the base and start seeing the town. I hadn't even begun working yet, and I already was regretting having to work. I was here to romp all over Europe; damn the Navy, I wasn't here for my career. After a half-hour, a woman came and walked me to where I'd be spending the next two years. It was a big yellow box of a building, with no windows but antennas and satellites all over the roof. Clearly something important went on in here, although I didn't have the first idea what.

I would be working on the second floor, although everyone called it the fourth floor, as there were two more floors below ground. It was your typical military office building: dull white walls and tiled floors, harsh bright lights, pictures of admirals, lots of flags, and walls plastered with asinine motivational posters - the kind that show a picture of an eagle or a jet fighter above meaningless phrases about leadership, perseverance, and determination.

Eventually I met my sponsor, a Lieutenant Public Affairs Officer. He was confident without being arrogant, and I could tell that in any situation this man knew exactly what he was doing. I could also tell that he both enjoyed his job and took it very seriously. Still, he didn't seem overbearing. I liked him immediately.

"Man, I am so sorry I wasn't at the terminal this morning; we didn't expect you for another month. This morning I'm sitting at my desk and the Commander calls me, 'Hey, you remember the guy you're sponsoring that's coming in April? I just walked him down to the Capo Inn.'"

I should have taken this as a bad omen and ran screaming from the building, but I knew I wouldn't be able to get back through the turnstile downstairs.

Eventually, I met the Navy Europe Public Affairs Officer and sat down in his office for the cookie-cutter "Welcome Aboard" speech - typically delivered when checking into a new duty station. I wasn't really sure what to make of him at first. He seemed nice but had a slightly wimpy disposition, and I could tell he got where he was by playing the system to the letter and never challenging it a bit. He had obviously spent a long time as a public affairs officer; his speech and mannerisms reflected someone used to speaking down politely to those he deemed beneath him. His office was a sterile white box with a dry erase board behind his desk that had all sorts of flow-diagrams, tasks, 'priorities' and to-do lists. His desk laid beneath a massive pile of unorganized paper work. A giant map of Europe hung on the wall, and the only things in there to indicate that someone actually occupied the space were a University of Nebraska baseball cap and the mini television upon which the cap rested.

"So, welcome aboard. Where are you coming from?"

"I was in San Diego, but I've spent the last two months in Virginia after a homeport shift."

"Oh, great, great. What was your job?"

"Weapons officer mainly, and supply, with about twelve other jobs thrown in."

"I see, I see. Great. Well, I think you'll fit in well here. You're joining us at a very exciting time. Morale's been a bit low recently, but it's really on the way up, and things are getting better around here all the time. Protocol should keep you very busy, and I think you'll find it to be an exciting and rewarding job."

"Well, I'm looking forward to the change of pace, sir; honestly, I'm just glad to be somewhere that doesn't get underway." I also was happy to be somewhere that I didn't need to put in much effort, but no need to let that little secret out just yet.

II

The next day I got settled into the Navy Lodge in Gricignano, a small town north of Naples where the Navy had leased property and built a large support facility. This 'mini-America' sported all the comforts of stateside living, including a large shopping center, commissary, gym, movie theater, high school and tons of government housing. A person could spend his entire tour here without ever setting foot onto proper Italian soil. Buses ran people to the bases in the area, so no one had to face the horrors of Italian driving; even local nationals working here spoke English, freeing everyone from having to learn even the most basic Italian. It was a monument to everything sick, greedy and isolated about our sheltered culture, everything that was wrong and spoiled-rotten about our lives, and I wanted nothing more than to see a large wrecking ball come demolish every building here.

Is this really what our tax dollars go towards? Given the state of turmoil across the globe and our over-extended military, is it really necessary to support mega-malls and bowling alleys that don't turn a profit? I understand the need to maintain morale and take care of families, but Italy isn't exactly a Third World country, and I can't imagine anyone being any worse off for going to an Italian grocery store once in a while. We Americans live our lives separated by two oceans from the rest of the world, blissfully ignorant of everything except what we're fed by sensational news programs. Whenever we're willing to go anywhere outside our country, we expect everyone to speak English and grant us all the best concessions by virtue of where we're from. We're only willing to experience the world via the Discovery Channel or from the windows of a tour bus.

Beyond my work, I wanted nothing to do with the people in this Americanized haven. I was going to commit the rest of my time in Naples to avoiding military contact as much as possible.

III

After performing my job for about a week, I started to get the idea of what 'protocol' meant: plan itineraries for visiting dignitaries, VIPs, admirals and generals, and the occasional Congressional delegation. This included setting up transportation and lodging, making restaurant reservations, setting seating arrangements and sending out invitations. Admirals like to throw parties at taxpayer expense - under a crafty little pocket of money known as Official Representation Funding - and protocol gets the dubious honor of organizing them. It's a job that requires a painful amount of attention to detail and scheduling, two things at which I have never been particularly good. The amount of time and effort put into a simple itinerary - not the content, mind you, but the format, font, and spacing of an Official Navy Instruction - would astound anyone. Many people pored over a document for hours before it was finalized, not because of a deep commitment to perfection or a hard-won work ethic that forbade mistakes, but because everyone with more than ten years of service had to 'chop' it to make sure that not one comma was out of place when the two-star admiral reviewed and signed it.

The people in protocol treated their jobs with an over-inflated sense of importance and lived their lives as though their balls were on the band saw at all times. As a result of my disgust for my unit, I became a shoddy performer at work - at least once a week I received lectures in my boss's white cube about things like The Mission and Details and Career. The meetings took place around six o'clock in the evening which required that I sit around until, in his words, he summoned me.

"I can't think of a single time in the past two weeks when I've walked by your office past sixteen thirty and seen you at your desk. Most of us are working 'til eight o'clock every night, and you're always outta here early. Are we not engaging you enough? Do you feel as though you're being allowed to contribute to the mission? Do you feel that what you're doing is unimportant? If that's the case, then let me know and we'll find work for you. The last thing you want is to leave here and not have anybody remember you."

"Well, sir, I'm always willing to stay late if need be - I did my time in engineering, and we were always there late - but if I finish my work for the day I don't really see the sense in sitting at my desk just for the sake of being there."

"That's just not good enough. We're all on the same team here, and you need to be taking some of the load off the others. Again, we're all here late every night; you need to be helping out the rest of the team, not running off on liberty early every day."

Now, I didn't see that my ability to manage my time and leave at a reasonable hour was indicative of laziness; it simply meant that I didn't want to work late, and that I didn't care to create work for myself. None of this mattered to my boss, a clock puncher who put more stock in hours logged than actual work done. I could come in early and work the same amount of hours as he, but all he would see in the end is that I was heading home at four and he was staying until eight. To him, that four hour window was the sole determinant of how hard one actually worked.

IV

My current job now seemed like a pathetic death rattle to a failed experiment at making myself a real Naval officer, and I wanted to be done with it. I didn't care what was next as long as I didn't have to 'salute the rank' and wear a uniform that I took no pride in anymore. I can clearly remember when I crossed the line from feeling good about my career choices and proud to serve, to a bitter, cynical old soul who looks back on a long chain of decisions and wonders just what the hell led me here in the first place.

I was on my first ship, in the Red Sea, when the fighting began in Iraq. I remember the days leading up to that point: the media frenzy, the heightened operational security, the tenseness of feeling that we were really going to war, and we'd be the first ones to participate. I didn't have a job on board - I spent the first six months learning about engineering and nothing else - and was more of

in those years we lived our best

an observer to the whole affair. Whether you agreed or disagreed with the decision to invade, it was very hard not to get caught up in the enthusiasm that we were going off to do big things. It was finally Our Turn, we were finally getting Our War, and for the old Cold War vets who had seen the buildup of the eighties turn to the drawdown of the nineties with nothing to show for it but pay cuts and smaller budgets, this was the greatest day of their lives. And so, that first night of 'Shock and Awe,' I stood in the pilot house and watched a seemingly endless display of bright orange streaks heading over the horizon to targets far away, a lethal fireworks display from ships all around us gathered for this historic day. I remember feeling very insignificant that day, not in a personal sense, but one that went along with being such a small part of a large operation, and I was glad to be there for it.

But then, after we had spent our load and completed our task, we were left to watch the events unfold on the television, wondering just what was next for us. That first hint of the regret monster began to rear its ugly head, and from that point on I couldn't help but feel like less of a man because others were genuinely going off in harm's way, fighting the real war, while we floated around in our comfortable gray hotel and impatiently awaited our next port visit. Our turn to play was over, and I felt all the more meaningless for it.

I don't mean to say I wish I had been on the ground at the time because of any belief in the justness of the cause; whether for or against invading Iraq, I would still rather have been participating. So many people my age were taking up arms and battling their way across the desert, why shouldn't I? Why wasn't I out there taking up arms with my brothers during the great conflict of our time? Had I forgotten all the things I had learned at The Citadel, those important lessons about trust and faith and fellowship, and always being there to back your brother's play no matter what? I felt empty and hollow inside, as though I had betrayed the guys on the ground by choosing to go to a ship instead of a platoon. How could I even say that I was there?

Simple, I can't and won't even try. And so now, while there is still fighting going on, while others my age - classmates and friends of mine, including some that have died - are carrying on in that endless arena of hate and destruction, I

quarter passed

sit at my desk and listen to the pointless ramblings of people that don't understand, and probably never will, that there are greater, more important things going on right now than anything we could ever hope to accomplish from this office. These bullshit artists and their sad, old ways, these careerists who value their own fitness reports over friendship and loyalty and could never even comprehend words like Honor, Brotherhood, and Sacrifice. Even for me, those words ceased to have meaning long ago, not because I forgot them, but because they rang hollow and empty whenever I tried digging them out of memory. Instead all that comes to mind are harsh words like Anger, Cynicism and Stupidity.

All I do now is hope that others share in my bitterness and frustration at the system as it stands. Maybe someone will stand up to the agenda pushers and faithless followers who have turned my Navy into a nightmare of lies and deceit. In the end, maybe I'll find my place in the world where I can go out and do something, anything of which I could be proud. I do work with people who are genuinely proud of what they do. They see themselves as pieces of a much bigger machine and are hard working, decent and dedicated, all those traits that give our military the potential to do great things. Unfortunately, I don't work for any of those people.

◆◆◆

bryan david blake. (26, naples, italy)

rhythm
by oluwagbemiga dasylva

The crack of dawn, noontime!
Not leaving the night… moment… age –
Add up to man's short existence
On this brittle orb, Rhythm!

You declare and dictate:
Man prances in a quagmire of dilemmas.
Cutting 'cross the ridge of stumpy requisites.
        Rhythm!

The English meter,
We call imi(s')ital[1]
I getting off the wall, they thought.
        Rhythm!

Isipaya[2]! They say 't is vision, puzzling!

    Makes me-   feel-   so
  dis-   joint-   ed

    How-do- I- get
    Your -hold-off-me?
        Rhythm!

You are life at noon-time; sunset your captivating dullness;
I live on Rhythms of the Sun. Your constant lilt.

1 *Yoruba expression for "breathe out"*
2 *Revelation or vision*

♦♦♦

oluwagbemiga dasylva. (23, oyo state, nigeria)

quarter passed

final 3. by alessandra mccune. (21, philadelphia, pennsylvania, usa)

3

self image

the smokers
by katherine prengel

You can usually spot a member of The Smokers' Club. Not in outward appearance, because The Smokers' Club is like a catch-all for those who otherwise do not like groups. No, our members can usually be found outside of office buildings and, in the sadder cities, bars and restaurants. And in our huddled groups, we utilize a language that is unique to us and to every individual within the group.

This is a language at once personal and universal. Like a mask which both shields the smoker and expresses, in archetypal fashion, a given attitude, the cigarette points up every conceivable emotion. I can demonstrate my sorrow, frustration, anger, and delight, all through the way that I hold my cigarette and the speed at which I smoke it.

If I light one cigarette after another, and put each one out before it is halfway smoked, then I am acting out my restlessness. If, on the other hand, I lean across a table to receive a light from the man who wants to buy me a drink, then I am of course expressing something totally different.

These are set gestures, understood by smokers everywhere. And, like all set gestures, they allow for infinite variations. My friends do not smoke in exactly the same way as I do, and everyone has his own method of putting out a cigarette. Nevertheless, within these variations the essential meaning remains clear.

Smokers are like mimes, performing a kind of constant street theater for one another. And just like mimes, they are slightly disguised. The unchanging nature of the cigarette, the formality of the accompanying gestures, make for a sheltering tradition, beneath which individuality is visible in small glimpses, as a face seen from the side, from behind a mask.

It is a special joy to smoke with people you know well, and to repeat again and again the same movements, sure of being understood. I light a second cigarette during my coffee break, and my friends know that I am still angry at our supervi-

quarter passed

sor; they all light second cigarettes around me in solidarity, and I grow happier among our cloud of smoke.

As much as they serve to express emotions, cigarettes are also the tools that a smoker uses to fix his feelings more firmly. This is difficult to explain. I am alone, listening to the radio, and suddenly the DJ puts on a song that I know and love. I jump up, happy; my body twists at the first bars of music, and I light a cigarette to draw out my pleasure. I smoke, and the very action of smoking makes the song peculiarly mine.

It is as though I have taken a huge pair of shears and cut five minutes out of time, making an isolated moment out of the cigarette and the song. Nothing else can intrude. I overlay this moment onto my morning, in the same way as I might paste a photograph into a letter to a friend. Time ceases to be a flat passage and comes to resemble a collage, made up of a series of brief, shining episodes, each the length of a cigarette.

The glory of smoking, then, is that it gives us the illusion of control - I can alter time itself - when, in reality, we smokers are ourselves the victims of one of the most powerful addictions known to man.

Not coincidentally, most smokers are people in positions of little power. The crowd around the office doors downstairs, smoking and shivering in the winter air, is made up of secretaries and mailroom clerks, while the managers and executives upstairs order healthy lunches, and do elaborate yoga stretches before meetings.

Why do we keep on smoking, then, as though the only way of altering reality is to kill ourselves slowly (and despite the Surgeon General's stern warnings)? Lung cancer and emphysema are no industry secrets. But they are also not effective deterrents.

I once quit smoking and found myself uncomfortably exposed to the universe, with no intermediary power to protect me. I imagine this is how religious people must feel, when they have a crisis of faith and can no longer believe in their god and in the intervening power of their saints.

And so, after months of not smoking in New York, I came to London and started up again. Every pack of cigarettes that I buy is printed with a big label

the smokers

that says, bluntly:

CIGARETTES KILL.

But I look at the warning, and, without meaning to, I let my eyes glaze it into a series of meaningless black shapes. I continue to act out my private and public dramas, smoking.

katherine prengel. (28, london, england)

quarter passed

apollo. by albert chi hwang. (26, san francisco, california, usa)

for me

by a.j. agnew

it's like a burning behind my eyes and i can't shake it
and it presses through everything i see
and it flattens everything around me
and i picture my eyes like dotted balloons
floating up and out
away and away
and they suddenly see everything i've ever wanted to

a.j. agnew. (26, kelowna, british columbia, canada)

quarter passed

twice. by marina bendet. (22, st. petersburg, russia)

being poor
by tracy bradley

I was fourteen when my dad left us and we became poor. The thing about becoming poor is that it is much more than a new state of finances - it is a new state of mind. You see the world in terms of how much things cost; everything has its price tag. You don't take the risks that others take, or maybe even those that you had taken before - flying off for a weekend in Cuba, for example. Even if you can afford life's luxuries, you want to be sure your bills are paid for the next six months.

Risk becomes frightening, not exhilarating, even if you're a person who normally loves to take risks. You don't see yourself as someone who can do things. You are crippled. You see yourself as someone who is poor. Who has to be careful. Keep track of each penny. Be watchful. It becomes the frame through which you see the world, and even if you are lucky enough to become not poor again, the viewpoint remains.

Even now, even though I am thirty, even though I am financially stable, I am poor in my heart. I do not feel okay, at ease. When I look in my fridge and see that it is full, I feel warm and safe. I am taking care of myself.

I survive by the cliché curse of the Formerly Poor: I spend my money on things. Clothes, so I don't ever look poor again. So I don't ever wear something used, or wear the same pair of jeans every day for a week because that's all I have in my closet. Domestics, for my flat, so it doesn't look poor. So it isn't cluttered with hand-me-downs, couches that require a bed sheet for camouflage, tables that wobble because one leg is broken but it's still good. Food, so that I never know what it's like to try and fall asleep on an empty stomach again. And, not only that, I buy the best food, expensive food, and I feel proud because I don't eat like a poor person. It didn't come from the donation box at my high school or church. It isn't food that other people decided they could do without.

quarter passed

It isn't poor food: No-Name canned beans, ramen noodles, macaroni and cheese. No Chef Boyardee for breakfast, lunch and dinner. No asking twenty people at school for a quarter each so I can buy something for lunch at 7-11, something that comes out of a plastic wrapper or a pump. I spend my money on evidence that I am not poor.

That is not living; it's a façade of my survival. I am no longer poor, but I am spiritually bankrupt.

It's hard to shake that feeling, though, that feeling that you have become the Other, that you have seen the worst of things. You are now different from your friends. Your identity becomes shaped: I am someone who struggles. Someone who manages. And it becomes real, and it becomes real forever - I can't do things because I am poor.

So you don't do things. You don't take the vacation because you might need to go to the dentist. You don't take the night course because two hundred dollars is a lot of money. You work at whatever job you need to work at to ensure that you're not poor, even if you find no interest in it, because interest is not as important as not being poor is. When you know how easily poverty can employ you, job satisfaction becomes meaningless.

So you become poorer still, as if you turned your pockets inside out but couldn't buy yourself happiness. And you wonder, sometimes, what that feeling is - that empty, longing, aching feeling that keeps you awake, that starts from your gut and snakes its way around your chest, gnawing a hole that grows deeper and more jagged with each passing paycheck.

You lay in your bed, covered in 400-thread-count Egyptian cotton sheets, and look around and wonder… why you are this way, why you have a head full of dreams that aren't going anywhere, why you haven't tried, and why you never put it together. You've lived your life never expecting to have. You've lived your life expecting to have-not. And that's exactly what's happened.

You expect the car to break down. You expect cracks to form in the walls. You expect holes in socks, dents in your credit, and short Christmas lists. You dream of bigger and better, but you don't ever really believe in bigger and better. So how can you take your own dreams seriously, seriously enough to pursue

being poor

them, to make them real, when you are so used to everything you want being just out of reach?

How do you get past that - even if it has been several years - and believe anything is possible when your existence is grounded in perpetual wanting? When you don't even realize that this has defined you? When you are the first generation who is NOT expected to do better than their parents, and your parents didn't do so well, how can something like writing a book or making a short film even seem possible?

John Scalzi wrote that being poor is running in place. I am not poor anymore. I am not rich, but I am not poor. Yet, I am still running - running from having been poor, and running to keep from ever being poor again. And I've been so busy running, I haven't gotten anywhere. I've been so busy running that I forgot to notice that I am, in fact, okay. That I can rest, finally, and enjoy life a little. That I am entitled to pursue my passions, to live rather than merely survive. I've been so busy running that I have crashed headlong into another type of poverty altogether. And I am forced to entertain the notion that perhaps poor is the only place I really feel safe.

tracy bradley. (30, toronto, ontario, canada)

quarter passed

untitled. by chris vialpando. (25, scottsdale, arizona, usa)

whiskey and fire

by lucy leitner

There is vomit in my sleeve and on the floor of the subway car. My apartment has brand new wall-to-wall carpeting. My eyes are bloodshot and my head is spinning. My office job gives me health care benefits. There is vomit in my hair that I just had cut earlier today for $60. There's a blistering cigarette burn on my arm. There are jeweled chandeliers in my apartment's lobby. There is something rotten in my life.

The attitude that less is more, that we don't need to ascribe our lives to a certain formula, strikes a harmonious chord within me - unless we are talking about sex, drugs and rock 'n' roll. I don't need wall-to-wall carpeting and a laundry room, a gym, and a convenience store in the basement. I don't need a doorman. I need something that will make me feel alive again. I need a risk, an adventure, a completely bizarre idea that will probably result in disaster.

Earlier tonight I picked up the bible of debauchery, *The Dirt*, the autobiography of the kings of heavy metal delinquency: Mötley Crüe. Tommy Lee, Vince Neil, Mick Mars and Nikki Sixx - four twisted souls who went from skid row to Shangri-La in a depraved carnival of sex, drugs, distorted guitars, destruction, audio terror, and utter insanity in a way that society condemns, like a drunken 100-mile per hour ride down the wrong way of a cobblestone one-way street. My life, on the other hand, is traveling under the speed limit with the parking brake on.

Tonight, I'm dressed nicely for a change - clad in a new H&M shirt, stomping along in Steve Madden stilettos. The only thing giving my true identity away is the tied-up fairy with nails through her wings tattooed on my back. Nothing else could reveal the whiskey and fire pumping through my veins. At work, in my little

quarter passed

cubicle, fact-checking at *U.S. News and World Report*, they don't know that, beyond my $140 Guess khakis and button-down shirt, a soundtrack of heavy metal has all my brain cells moshing and breaking shit inside my head.

A knock on the door forces me to put down the heavy metal lifestyle bible, but not without an epiphany: I used to be fun. I used to go to class in leather pants. Earlier today, I cut about four inches off my hair. Technically it looks better, but right after I did it, I couldn't believe I could have so callously betrayed my 80's metal tenets in such a foul and sacrilegious manner. I am not Samson, but I stand to lose all my strength. What is happening to me?

I open the door and let Leila and Kara into my apartment, which is bereft of soul, but stocked with stylish furniture and once-unimaginable luxuries like a dishwasher, a garbage disposal, and a refrigerator stocked full of healthy choices. I don't drink milk, so I'll get osteoporosis and my teeth will fall out.

Rockers Cinderella say, "You don't know what you've got 'til it's gone." Well, I had nothing and I want it back. Actually, I had an apartment where I was allowed to hang up my movie villain paintings. And I had people who could laugh when we were so broke we bought individual slices of cheese from the deli. Is it weird that I miss the smell of cat shit, stale cigarettes, old beer, and pizza grease? I've already been drinking. I drink, so I'll destroy my liver and wreck my brain.

Leila and Kara sit down at the dining room table (because apparently it is necessary for proper twenty-two year-old girls - I mean, ladies - to have a separate dining room area). I'm serving a buffet, a random assortment of shit from the liquor store, and an urge comes over me to write a "blaxploitation" flick and cast Kara, our African Queen, as my lead.

Leila's last name is Baghdadi and we used to steal liquor from her parents after their annual Eid parties at the end of Ramadan. I'm Jewish. The three of us thrive on misconceptions, the liberal, post-9/11 wet dream, a group so diverse can be so close and overlook ethnic differences to bond on a more profound level.

A few years ago we invented a drinking game that entails naming a racial slur for each letter of the alphabet. "U" always had us stumped until I had a stroke of brilliance with "Uncle Tom". Some would say this game is degrading as

whiskey and fire

Leila, our token Muslim, cites "Ragheads", but what are we to do?

My roommate Olivia returns home to join in the drinking binge, the Southern belle, the Catholic schoolgirl whose mother pulls in six hundred grand a year. She's got a $20,000 trust fund, "just in case." When Nikki Sixx was our age, he was selling light bulbs on the phone while trying to put a band together. He was living in a hellhole with no food, sleeping on the living room floor, stepping over people who were fucking for blow and a spot in the scene. They lived to die young, reckless indulgence, creating a ruckus all the while.

Me? I hide my tattoos to abide by office dress codes and mingle with successful people who actually wanted to live in a nice apartment at twenty-two. I miss my old life: dead broke, finding innovative ways to cook Ramen, struggling to do what I wanted, never taking the easy road to boredom.

I miss the days when I walked a mile to the gym just to shower because my gas got shut off and I had no hot water. Now there's a gym in the bottom of my building and there was a huge crisis when the garbage disposal broke. Where is my comfortable world of chaos?

Kara and I go out to the massive balcony to smoke five cigarettes each. I smoke, so my lungs will go black and I'll lose my sense of taste.

I finish a 24-ounce bottle of Corona while we try to agree upon an agenda for the evening, a bar where we can all have fun; where Leila and Kara can booty dance, where Olivia can pick up guys with dark hair, where I can accomplish my mission.

I have not yet revealed my intentions to the others, for fear that I'd be met with looks of haunting disapproval and utter confusion. But to me, the plan is simple; I will get so completely wasted tonight that I will do something ridiculous and destructive, and I will blame it all on that damn Mötley Crüe book pushing me over the edge. I will drink whiskey. One of my tattoos is exposed and there is no way I'm hiding it tonight. I get tattoos, so I'll get hepatitis and regret it when my skin wrinkles, if I live that long.

I always have been (and I always will be) completely obsessed with rock 'n' roll and it permeates everything that I do (as it has since I was fourteen). And tonight, I'm going to give into it. There are worse things to be addicted to. My

quarter passed

first favorite song was by Steppenwolf. I was a victim of heavy metal blood poisoning in the womb. I listen to Judas Priest, so I'll kill myself, and I listen to Marilyn Manson and Helter Skelter so I'll kill everyone else.

Already buzzing, we take off to the subway to head out for the evening. I ride subways, buses, trains, and planes, so I'll be killed by terrorists.

It's around 11 p.m. and my other roommate, Ashley, is probably asleep by now at her parents' house. Or, she's knitting, and bemoaning the yearlong loss of her fiancé to Korea, narrowly missing an army assignment to Iraq in favor of a longer hardship tour. She knits afghans, works her mindless job six days a week for overtime pay, cooks (always according to a recipe), lives in self-assigned domestic hell, a housewife with two female roommates her own age. She cooks chicken florentine and cheeseburger pie and has become addicted to baking lasagna. With all this Botox and anti-wrinkle cream and the obsession with eternal youth, why is everyone surrounding me so prematurely middle aged?

Everything that was intriguing about Ashley in high school - that she would come into class and intelligently degrade the pompous assholes while wearing a feather boa and handing out home-baked cupcakes for no reason - has given way to pristine normality. The only trace left of her former flamboyance is the pair of gold pants banished to the depths of her messy closet. Now she's a pale skeleton, popping Zoloft and eleven other pills a day to make herself feel normal.

Olivia's on anti-depressants for anxiety attacks. The only pill I take is Zantac because I drank too much in college and gave myself acid reflux. Where did all this shame of one's own little flaws come from? I miss my friend Matt, who refused to take his prescribed Aderol, and my old roommate Ronan, who stopped taking Paxil cold turkey because it interfered with his partying. I miss people who don't need drugs to feel normal. I miss people who don't want to be normal.

Maybe that's why all the top-grossing movies of the last five years have been sequels or adaptations or remakes; we've drugged-out all the originality. I'm not comfortable here, with this life, but I'll never take pills to numb myself into mild acceptance. Nikki Sixx wouldn't have either. The real me is completely ignorant of current trends in entertainment. Give me 80's metal and 70's horror flicks any day.

whiskey and fire

We exit the subway station and flag down a cab to get us nearer to the bars. I lift my upper torso out the window, cigarette in my mouth, and sit on the window ledge so half my body feels the winds that we cut through at 50 MPH.

Kara screams, "Niggers!" out the front window. It seems fitting that, our very "politically correct" group needs a black woman to call pedestrians "niggers" for no reason.

The cab stops at the bars and I climb out the window without opening the door, miraculously landing on the sidewalk without eating cement. Olivia thinks I'm insane, but this is my first step to doing everything wrong. Recently even weekends have become routine around here; a bar, a few drinks, taking the puking roommate home, going to sleep by 2 a.m., followed by grocery shopping and *Sex and the City* reruns the next day.

At twenty-two, I'm already becoming an old woman. Maybe my computer will break and I'll be stuck living again. Maybe the cable will die or a freak lightning bolt will electrify the TV and we'll be forced to go out and live real lives, or at least ones less intertwined with the characters of *CSI*.

Since I have already exhibited a stealth desire to do what I want tonight, my friends do not object when I drag them into Asylum, a cavernous biker bar where Mötley Crüe's "Dr. Feelgood" is blaring when we walk in. I listen to loud music, so I'll go deaf.

I order a beer and rock out to speakers blasting my own feelings set to music written by someone else. I can feel the minor dissociative effects of alcohol working as my left hand crunches into Ronnie James Dio's legendary devil horns. My brain tries to prevent the transformation, but there's nothing it can do. Bon Scott salutes me from the grave. I smash the obligatory beer can against my forehead. I live for this shit.

My huge, blond curls look much better with leather than a blazer. I can pull off office chic during the day, but tonight I am free to be myself. Ashley and Olivia look like nice, pretty girls. I'm covered in scars and my hair dye job is totally botched. There is paint on the majority of my clothing and holes in the rest. My teeth are not perfectly straight (nor white), my never-manicured nails are short, and I wouldn't have it any other way. I don't floss my teeth, so

quarter passed

they'll decay and I'll have to replace them with gold so I can join a rap posse and get shot.

I'm in the bathroom, so I don't see Olivia and Kara make out at the bar over their rum and diet cokes. Had I just seen them as strangers, the old me would have called them morons and had to refrain from smashing their empty heads into their bitch drinks. Instead, I order another whiskey and coke with full calories because I don't believe in mixing drinking and dieting. I'm an American, so I'll get fat.

For some reason, I offer to put a cigarette out on my arm so Leila will buy me a beer. The Marlboro Light brands a perfect circle into my flesh and it doesn't really hurt as much as I would have believed. Iggy Pop and G.G. Allin may not have been that tough after all.

Olivia has just pounced on the man she's been ogling for the past few minutes, one of the other few low-key preppies in the moderately crowded bar mostly frequented by tattooed patrons of diverse musical taste. It's in this scene that I feel most comfortable; like the dive bars we'd hit in Pittsburgh, drinking Iron City and shots of Jägermeister with college dropouts, bartenders, mediocre bands, and tattoo artists. Why, after being raised in such an upper middle class area, do I have such a fascination with a culture borne out of white trash?

Are we really the first downwardly mobile generation? Maybe we have to be; there will be no American Dream for me, for my parents already accomplished it. I never had rags, so how can I go to riches? Maybe I should have nothing, so that I can move up in the ranks and really feel like I earned it, rather than rising through my mother's connections. (I still ended up with a job that can barely afford my rent in the spacious apartment with a view and a balcony and a parking spot.) If we were born with everything, wouldn't we want nothing at least for a while? Devolution. A soup kitchen future for the rich, like in a Chuck Palahniuk novel.

My roommate is now in coquettish, moronic conversation with the guy. She's upset she hasn't gotten laid in a few weeks. In my old group, where I felt so at home, it was pretty much a prerequisite that we give up sex. Not for any moral reason, but because when engaging in the ridiculous brand of fun that we were so addicted to, it was a given that no one would want to fuck us. And we didn't care.

I can feel myself slipping away into the intellectual abyss of drunkenness, and boredom is taking over as Olivia is occupied by her prey and Leila and Kara have gone next door to dance to hip hop for a while. I buy another drink and light another cigarette, harassing the DJ to play W.A.S.P., but he doesn't have them, so I demand Hanoi Rocks, Skid Row, Guns n' Roses, more Mötley Crüe, or anything that gets me away from here and now. I am not meant to mingle with lawyers and Congressmen.

The encroaching boredom is becoming intolerable, so I approach the long-haired dude who's dancing like a moron on the opposite side of the pool table. My greatest fear is boredom. My life would be so much easier if it was filled with zombies. I hear myself having the same conversation over and over with him and his friend, who tell me they're in a band so I pretend to be interested.

Just months ago, I could go out with my three closest friends in Pittsburgh and speak to no one but them and we'd all have the time of our lives. We're each other's desert island people there. Here, I am on nobody's island, and no one here is on mine. I look over at Olivia and she's having a ball. I'm having a breakdown.

I'm not registered to vote. Why the fuck do I live near Washington, D.C.? I don't read the magazine I work for. Come to think of it, I don't read any news at all, except updates on Axl Rose's elusive *Chinese Democracy* album.

I want to live in a haunted castle, not behind a white picket fence. I want to relive the days of accidentally setting myself on fire. I want to wonder where I'll be in six months. I want to live in a hellhole and spend money on booze and hairspray. I want a roommate who doesn't only like my art when she's drunk. I want to bring the real me back for more than blurry cameos in drunken nights on the town. I don't want to watch *Sex and the City* anymore. I'd rather be a carnie, or a bounty hunter, or a freelance armed robber. I am not a twentysomething career girl, thriving on happy hours or office parties. I don't mingle or schmooze. I don't have a glass of wine with dinner. I don't own a vibrator. I own a karaoke machine. I drink Mad Dog 20/20 straight from the bottle.

quarter passed

Lita Ford sang, "I went to a party last Saturday night. I didn't get laid, I got in a fight," back in 1987 – but I could swear, twenty years later, that she stole what's in my head.

Olivia is still wrapped up in conversation with her love of the night. His short hair is covered by a baseball cap and he's dressed up in a GAP sweatshirt. When my dream man walks into a room, you can hear a soundtrack of sex-drenched metal from days past. He spits whiskey and breathes fire. I'm not too sure he exists. But if he does, I'll find him. I won't settle for the first pretty face in a bar. I may die alone.

Leila and Kara have returned from ghetto superstardom, informing me that it is time to go and I don't resist. We walk out of the bar and I throw myself on the dirty sidewalk and begin to swim. My friends do not find this as amusing as I do, so they hail a cab and as soon as it starts moving, I find that earth's rotation speed has increased exponentially. Olivia is cuddled up to her pretty boy and I am trying to keep myself awake. When the cab arrives at the subway, seemingly hours later, I jump out and lunge into a Washington Post box, beating the inanimate object to the ground. Take that, you current event motherfucker! Demolish the political media of this town! Rock 'n' roll, heavy metal, motherfuckers! Die yuppie scum! Shout at the devil!

My friends quickly usher me into the subway station and onto the train. My head is hung low and I know I have lost. Alcohol has beaten me, destroyed the last inkling of hope for the rest of my ridiculous evening. I feel my eyes close, shielding me from the spinning subway car. But suddenly, when I think my body can't keep up with my rebellious mind, it happens, something more ludicrous than I would ever have expected.

Vomit spews from my mouth into my sleeve, onto the empty seat next to me, onto the floor of the moving train, and all over my new, trendy jeans. Hah, take that metropolitan transit system! Even covered in stomach acid, that whiskey will make you start banging your head, you goddamn train. I doubt this is what Nikki Sixx would do, but I'm sure he'd approve of my efforts twenty years later than when I should have lived.

I'll work for a while in a coffee shop where it won't be taboo for me to have that half-sleeve tattooed on my arm like I've wanted forever. I'll keep selling my horror movies for five-hundred bucks a pop on the side and continue writing art reviews for local magazines. I'll live in a shit-hole apartment where the bathroom wall is rotting off and, if I get really desperate, I'll sell my soul on eBay. Maybe I'll go to Hell, but I'd rather be there anyway because the devil has better musical taste. Besides, I've always imagined it to look a lot like a Kiss concert, so how bad could it be? Maybe in a decade's time I'll be ready to grow old.

I give one final hurl on the train floor, just to show who's the boss. This should not be my release. I am grown up and ready to take on the world, to give it my all, even if right now all I'm giving is a terrible mess for some unassuming subway worker to clean up in the morning. I have fun, so I'll die young.

lucy leitner. (22, arlington, virginia. usa)

quarter passed

melencolia. by emilie mae bezaire. (21, smyrna, tennessee, usa)

how to lighten a heavy load

by gena mavuli

I carry the weight of this city on my thick sturdy calves
leaving my ankles pulsing with the blood of this saturated town
swollen with passion, tears, and early morning runs
towards the morning moon

Exhausted at the end of the day
unable to place where my energy has gone
realize that I've been spreading it over town,
blanketing the city in as much of me as I can
so that it'll remember me when I want to return
in this one place I won't be a foreigner

Smoke after work, cigarettes and beer, vices
co-workers return to their spouses,
left alone with the evening, me and The Night
relish in endless romantic hours as we stroll through time
my neighborhood and I go home together,
rest with our bodies luxuriously tangled
a casual, soft knot

Sleep and absorb energy from the midnight moon
that lights up my modest home.
The days keep coming, demanding more of me
and I open up and pour my heart again onto the streets,
into the people in my own silent goodbye

quarter passed

Dance in a club too late on a Wednesday night
spin, glide, laugh, follow, trip, smile, hold on tight
step, twirl and soar through the early hours of the morning
leaving my scent in the air, at the bar,
on shirts of heated partners
my remnants slowly drive all these tired bones home
collapse into bed with throbbing feet,
wake up too soon
smelling like men, sweat
tasting the sweet salt of my life

I love cool drizzly nights full of rich beer and pure laughter.
Swim in pain heartache joy elation
cry with the power of Zeus

I sleep soundly
beside someone, anyone
best friend, lover, companion
socks and underwear strewn about the room
wine glasses on the windowsill glow in early morning light

I love waking up alone
Smelling last nights smoke in my tousled hair,
sweat on my tacky skin
the scent of every man I ever knew

I love the way I'm saying goodbye,
the smell of Portland in the spring

❖❖❖

gena mavuli. (27, buenos aires, argentina)

untitled. by laura elena soria pineda. (29, mexico city, mexico)

quarter passed

dances with stars
vicky puzon-diopenes

Once upon the sky
Ablaze with stars it gazed upon
My loveliness my smile.
And once upon the stars I slept
and dreamed and played and danced.
Yet, reality takes its royal throne,
I fall, cascading like a shooting star...
and down upon the dust of dirt and mire and muck
I weep.
Morning breaks and green the grass when dew does shine
God lifts up my soul and I...
I learn to inhale dawn's first breath, drawing in earth's saving air.
All day long, I live upon the soil - I see the lilies and the bumblebees,
The footsteps in the muddy ground.
I raise my eyes up and see the trees
Their upper arms embracing the silver specks...
I am... gazing on stars once more...
Not to go the distance and dwell in the heavens
Not to climb the highest peak and reach out to the glitter
But to sit admiringly from afar,
Remembering the dances I once danced in the luminous sparkle.
But stars are not meant to hold one such as me,
I am my destiny fulfilled,
As my feet land safely - I dance and dance - on the earth.

by vicky puzon-diopenes. (30, pathum thani, thailand)

happy anniversary

by corey podell

One Year Anniversary. I've never had an anniversary of any sort. I feel relatively good today; I lost a couple pounds this week, and I'm wearing the blue dress and boots that I like. He made a reservation at the fancy sushi restaurant where we had our first date. I'm home too late. We miss the reservation. It doesn't bother either of us. We'll go somewhere else on that street. Fine.

The restaurant a block up is full, too. We cross the street. Fancy Korean restaurant. I've never had this kind of food before.

"Is this place okay?" he asks me; I say sure.

What a silly question, I think to myself, I'll eat anything.

We walk in, it's really fancy. I worry, can we afford it? Oh well, it's our anniversary.

The fancy hostess seats us at a beautiful table with impeccable lighting and then leaves us to the menus. He talks about his day at work and his asshole boss. I look at him and react intermittently, all the while tuning him out as I think about what I will order that won't make me feel full, bad, anxious. I don't think about what I would like to taste, I haven't thought about that in years. I just need to control the aftermath.

We look at the menu. I see fish. That's good; I'll order fish, safe choice. No guilt there. I feel a moment of relief. I have control; I have a plan; I know what I'm going to do. GOOD, I can tune back in to my anniversary dinner. The waiter comes. We order wine. Only one glass, Corey; if you have more, you'll want to eat more, lose more control. Drink it slow. I order my fish, he orders a Korean sampler, which is a bunch of different small dishes, AND vegetable tempura as an appetizer.

quarter passed

I feel a moment of panic. That's a lot of food coming to our table. I almost say something, but then I realize that the moment of panic has morphed into a little excitement - he ordered something I'm looking to forward to trying. He always does without even knowing it.

We talk about our day. He's talkative tonight; that's good, usually he's very quiet. I'm hungry. The wine comes, and then the tempura. I eat one piece; its good. I'm glad he ordered it. I eat another. That's ok, I tell myself. It's only vegetables, right? Fried vegetables. I eat more. He eats some. There is one piece left, he asks me if I want it - I say no. He eats it and I wish I had said yes.

I do a "check in" - something that fancy nutritionist I used to see told me to do from time to time. Yep, I'm already feeling pretty full.

The Korean sampler comes. Oh my god, there are about twenty tiny dishes. He and I try each one together and decide if we like it or not. They are all pickled vegetables or fish. That's fine, right? Just vegetables, just fish, small bites. I keep eating, eating the ones I've decided that I like. I'm pretty full. Stop eating! Why can't you stop? Just stop! I keep putting my chopsticks down and folding my hands in my lap. I decide to stop. Try to talk to him. Pick them up again, keep going. One more bite, just one more. I'm full. I haven't heard a word he's said for the past ten minutes.

The waiter comes back, has something in his hand - the fish I ordered. Forgot that I ordered the fish. Shit. Can I just take it to go? No, I want to try a bite right now. Amazing, this is the best fish I ever had, truly. I make him try it, and he agrees. I take a few more bites of the delicious fish. Why didn't I save myself for this fish? I'm angry that I made myself so full on other things. Why didn't I control myself? Okay, stop, you can take the rest home. Another bite. Stop it. Another bite. STOP. My stomach hurts. I'm in a horrible mood now.

I wonder what their bathroom is like. Is it a single? Let me go check it out. I stand up, walk to the bathroom, and pass a mirror on the way. YUCK, I can almost see how my stomach is bigger, maybe it's a mind trick, but I know I can see it, the weight I just put in my body.

The bathroom is a single. Relief floods my body. All my anxiety is gone. I don't do anything yet. I'll come back in a little while. Reapply lip gloss; walk

happy anniversary

back to the table. I feel in control; now I really have a plan. Now that I know there is a way out, I finish the delicious fish. Because I can. He tells me what a great anniversary this was, I agree. He tells me I look pretty; I tell him to shut up. He laughs. When there is no food left I take a sip of water. Excuse myself again, he asks if I'm okay. Of course.

My return to the bathroom. I do it. All that I ate leaves my body. I feel better, almost euphoric, complete and total relief. There was so much, I ate so much.

My return to the table - clarity, relaxation on my walk back. Disappointment, disgust, shame as I look at my sweet boyfriend admiring me. Clueless. I can't even look at him.

We pay the bill, we leave.

Happy Anniversary.

corey podell. (25, los angeles, california, usa)

quarter passed

imagen. by constanza fontenla. (24, buenos aires, argentina)

4
relationships and sex

men / women. by sarah hamilton. (25, vancouver, british columbia, canada)

quarter passed

confessions of a southern hustler

by b.h. shepherd

a eulogy for decorum and all things sacred

    The Pope is dead, but it's still Saturday night on Peach Tree Boulevard. Downtown Athens is dressed to the nines and full of booze when we receive word. The infallible has fallen, and the air fills with a profound sense of "What now?" My dear friend and accomplice in most things illicit, La Chinita (as she is known in her circles of operation) is frantically phoning and consoling every fellow Catholic she can as she teeters on the brink of a mojito-fueled meltdown herself.

    "MY POPE DIED!" As a convert from a Buddhist family, La Chinita had adopted Catholic history as a lengthy footnote to her own rich heritage. She was shaken by the death of the only pope she had ever known, the pope who had sold her on this whole Catholic gig in the first place. A nation of the faithful teetered on the edge of an uncertain future without a leader, and there were fears that a schism might be in store. With the progression of the modern age in the Western world, well-intentioned liberalism has replaced militant morality. Will no one ever speak for the center? It's hard to be a human being. It can be comforting to wrap yourself in Catholicism, like a warm blanket, centuries of tradition assuring you you're no worse than the rest. I like to remind everyone that, according to those freaky books that people insist are actual divine manuals of existence, we are all sinners.

    We have just come from a birthday party for the soul of Marvin Gaye at Little Kings, where DJ Mahogany spins everything from Ray Charles to Wu Tang. Bars choke with mourners tying one on for John Paul and street musicians draw showers

confessions of a southern hustler

of change from emotional drunks for a few bars of "Every Rose Has Its Thorn" on banjos and harmonicas. La Chinita surrenders her phone and we retreat into The Firehouse, just another college-town dive where the bars are for dancing because the regulars show up two sheets to the wind; but tonight is something truly special.

Normally my accomplice and I would be overdressed for the occasion in a white leisure suit and pink pinstripes on black silk, respectively, as we are fond of doing; the only thing better than looking good is looking too good. But The Firehouse is a different affair altogether. Tonight's crowd glitters like fine silver on a vinyl tablecloth. The university students are dressed in purple velour jumpsuits and impeccably white kicks for the annual Player's Ball, bumping, grinding, and drinking to a numbing bass line and the garbled drone of some studio gangster. La Chinita is already on the bar, a tiny Asian girl lost to the beat, thrashing it out with a cocktail in one hand and a brass-topped cane in the other. A partner is superfluous at this point; I learned long ago to just hand her a bottle of tequila and turn on the radio, hoping that somewhere out there 50 Cent was earning a royalty.

No one has come to the Player's Ball to see me shake my ass on the bar, so I focus on the real task at hand; acquiring whiskey and grabbing the attention of one of these lovely Southern gals for "research." That was the true purpose of this whole trip, the mad pursuit of answers; answers that had eluded me one slush-balled Thursday morn in upstate New York, as I struggled to make sense of some whiskey scrawl hacked on the page in angry block letters from nights previous, a frustrated hand that can only be writing about a woman. Indecipherable as it may be, I still know what's there, having written it many times before but never finishing, a scene that repeats itself endlessly with the tragic precision of Sisyphus' rock. Bar after bar, night after night, pretty girls draw me in like a moth to a flame. Think for a moment not about the cliché, but about the moth, at long last achieving his goal, finally wrapping his wings around that beautiful light he just could not resist.

An example? Very well.

Two-dollar pitcher night is never a good place to get a date. It's a great

quarter passed

place to pick up women. The lady of Thursday morning's scrawl was a white-blouse faded-jean post-grad intellectual with cool green eyes boxed up in a pair of librarian's glasses. I told her she looked smart. She said it was all an act and I conceded it was very convincing; could I get her a drink? Her clothes looked fresh out of the dryer and her hair was a bouquet of herbal shampoo, but there was also the unapologetic smell of cigarettes which meant the lady was drinking my drink: whiskey and a whiskey. She let half a smile slip and a fantasy unfolded of us closing out the bar in a whiskey-fueled literary debate, scrawling cocktail poetry in cheap notebooks and on each other, waking up to do *The New York Times* crossword puzzle in bed.

A traditional courtship might be likened to a game of cat and mouse, the boy and girl communicating their intentions through a rich and subtle play of manners as they pursue and resist each other. But the prelude to getting laid in the Northeast (only couples go on "dates" anymore) is more like a street fight; you use every dirty trick you know to subdue your opponent before it's too late. Every bit as romantic as it sounds.

Rarely do two strangers exchange three such perfect lines, and I'm determined to use the advantage while it is mine, calculating what move or phrase to use next. As a Texan and a gentleman I'd be disgusted with myself for thinking this way, for turning a pleasant conversation with a pretty girl into a game of strategy, but four years of college has trained me for a brutal hunt.

My generation inherited the fallout of the Sexual Revolution, leftover ideology from kids who proudly stood up to their parents' twisted traditionalist regime of modesty and monogamy. But what we got was an inbred mutant cousin of Free Love – the hookup culture, a true social meat-market.

A generation of youngsters with rebellion in their veins raised by parents who accepted and even approved of pre-marital sex. How do you rebel against that? Sex is "okay" and even "understandable" if you're just two dumb kids in love. Fuck that, Mom and Dad, we can fuck for the hell of it; fuck love! We're cute when we're defiant, but our sexual identity has been defined by icons of promiscuity, the lineups of *90210* and *American Pie*, groups of kids who switch partners like they're at a square dance, and for whom a "date" is just a means to an end (the slowest one). We've forgotten that the primary reason to buy a lady's dinner is for the pleasure of her company whilst you dine. In a post-Kinsey and Carrie Bradshaw society, sex is a commodity traded amongst the young; you just have to know how to broker the deal.

Simple pleasantries and small talk no longer hold the shy promise of intimacy, but the hollow ring of a transaction being completed. My smart Saratoga librarian, for instance. Soon we would be trying to squint our way through the Times, I was sure, clever puns and sly innuendos over breakfast. Only a fantasy, I never cook breakfast, but in the middle of it her defensive line steps in; a friend tugs on her arm. Their ride was waiting.

New York ladies (the single ones, that is) try to keep each other single. You'll know immediately if you picked the trophy (every group has one) because two of her friends will remind her that they were gonna go soon and it's getting late. My trophy Saratogan librarian said she was waiting on a drink. She then asked me to buy her 20-year old friend a drink. I told her I couldn't. It would violate my parole.

Had I said "yes," it would've been awkward trying to get rid of the friend, making a quick exit out the front door or even a second-story window. But that's the game in the Northeast; no matter how hot the sex is, the connection is anything but warm.

The hookup is a new, modern phenomenon. I recall an old mentor's lurid tales of Skidmore's girls-only days, when busloads of Union men came to campus every weekend like sailors on shore leave. Sexcapades aside, they all still had a girl, that someone special. So what could explain the stunning absence of courtship rituals in my generation? Relationship milestones are measured in how often you sleep together rather than how many dates you've been on. Everyone builds stables of "reliable" hookups and fuck-buddies. Perhaps our sexual forbears were not less promiscuous, just more discreet. But discretion has been rendered obsolete, deemed too oppressive and old-fashioned. No one is even sure what you mean anymore when you use the word "date", a sure sign that the old order has finally toppled.

I've come to Georgia to prove myself right about the South's grand tradition of courtship; that decorum may be unfashionable but still functional. Now if only I could find a lady for research. I'm still waiting on the bartender in Athens when across the bar, beyond the bared legs, leopard fedoras, and costume bling, a curious country blue eye catches mine.

It belongs to a quiet blonde, real calendar-girl material, the kind that makes you wish there were fifteen months in a year. She's wearing tear-away sweats and a tube top, but there are diamonds in her ears.

I grab the bartender, "Whiskey and a Cosmo for the belle at the end of the bar; you'll know when you see her." The DJ scrapes the bottom of his crate and hits a layer of the 80s, old dirty hip-hop that sets The Firehouse whistling as the snow white crowd remembers the golden age of MTV, grinding with renewed offbeat fervor. I'm scanning the bartop for my accomplice when behind me I hear the unmistakable ruckus of an empty cocktail glass.

"I need a drink!" La Chinita wails, leaning on her cane for support, emotional rather than physical. The intense white-knuckle grip on the brass seems to be the only thing holding back tears of alcohol. She sees me and pounces, burying her face in my chest as she cries out in the metaphysical agony of spiritual loss. I remember that the Pope has just died.

I hand my whiskey off to La Chinita, who gulps it down like water as I nod across the bar at the lady enjoying her Cosmo. La Chinita sees her, we exchange looks, I pucker my lips and all is understood.

"Give me five and room to breathe," I tell La Chinita, "She's got information I need."

My subject is on her way over, pink drink in hand like a signal flag, as La Chinita takes to the bartop, screaming at the DJ for some Usher. Doesn't he know who died? I leave my accomplice to her devices to focus on my own, like appearing not to notice the ghetto-fabulous Southern belle sidling up to me like a nervous schoolgirl. She asks how I knew her favorite drink and I say something about buying a pretty drink for a pretty girl, thanks for indulging me.

But neither of those is true. To make a distance pickup like this one you have to rely on the drink to do the talking for you; lines don't work when you have to yell them. With a simple beginner's course in bartending you can learn to size up a lady's liquor tastes simply by her clothes and her smell. Cigarettes covered up with perfume means a vodka tonic, or whiskey and water in the South. If her appearance looks to require more than ten minutes of assembly, daiquiris and margaritas are the way to go. And for diamonds, you always order up a Cosmo.

It's not an exact science, but it's a more than effective theorem. Small talk is easy after that, because she's already associated you with the delicious and intoxicating beverage. Conversation is how you lure the mouse out of the hole. But even if she comes over, remember she can still walk away. Let the lady talk; the goal is to keep her engaged while making her comfortable with you. Contrary to popular belief, this is not as difficult as it sounds if you just follow a simple formula: confidence plus wit times mystery, divided by safety, equals doable.

$$\frac{(C+W)*M}{S} = D$$

Every player's game has its own unique signature, like a musician's own unique style. How you play the game is up to you, which is why many single ladies on the circuit have a template of an abstract Mr. Wrong, compiled through bitterly recounted experience, that they have either cured themselves of, or wish they could. Or they haven't met him yet, but optimism like that sends you home to an empty bed, and who wants that?

Take the Cosmo Girl, for example. She comes over to find out who knew her favorite drink. A solid white tie with just the right amount of drawl betrays class around these parts. Wit can't be learned, only practiced, but the veneer of confidence can be counterfeited with astonishing ease.

Confidence can be the game-winning card if you play it at just the right moment, provided she doesn't call your bluff, like when her fella comes around, curious who she's talking to. With eyes on the prize, casually hand him a ten and tell him to relax and go get a drink. When he protests hand him another and tell him to buy two, all the while praying the lady doesn't want another Cosmo for convincing. But she doesn't; she's after a number, a name, a place, anything to validate her connection to this charming stranger. What takes place between two

quarter passed

sinners behind closed doors is no one's business in Georgia.

My conscience is screaming for attention when there's some bad noise up on the bar and the conga line is shattered. A polished piece of brass breaks above the crowd and comes down with a golf-like swoosh that cuts through the bass like a switchblade. I did not witness the ass-grabbing that La Chinita screamed about as she clawed at the Abercrombie hustler, but I have no doubt that it had occurred. White pants had always been her curse.

The poor fool recoils with a wounded dog whimper, holding his eye as La Chinita demands an apology. Didn't he know better than to just grab a lady? Indeed, didn't any of us know better? Weren't we all ashamed of ourselves, drinking to excess, lying to women, starting fights and groping nice ladies without a proper introduction?

Alas, there was no time for guilt as I abandoned the belle and pushed my way through the crowd to the scene of the crime, for I saw the injured player had backup, an Aryan linebacker with a clock hanging from his neck and his fist cocked to throw a right. My only thought was that I had to save him, for little Chinita had years of hand-me-down military training, the gift of a loving father. I yelled that his friend got exactly what he deserved, and didn't bother to add that she had plenty left for him as well.

But it was to no avail. I came back to the South to prove that things were not as bad as they seemed, but the whole time I was only learning the hard way, the only way we kids ever learn anything. The linebacker puckers his face into a "fuck you," but chokes on the syllables when I elbow him in the throat and shove him to the floor; any and all hopes for order and a peaceful resolution to anything are lost and I'm ready for the nosedive into chaos.

Everything we respected is dead, all that is left for us is empty-headed violence and shallow sex, a generation of endorphin junkies begging each other for a hit. We tore down the dam, but replaced it with nothing. The water has stagnated.

Out of nowhere the bouncer starts doing his job and the aggressive energy of the whole mess breaks on him. He sees me barely holding back the irate La Chinita and yells at me to get her out of here, pointing to the back door.

confessions of a southern hustler

"This is an outrage," I have no problem telling him. "You throw those abercrombienaziscum out too, or I'll turn her loose on you. How good's your dental?" His face tightens, but he decides against it and signals his partner over to help take out the trash. I give my best shit-eating grin and escort my accomplice out the fire doors at the back into a thick and sweaty Georgia night, streets full of sinners checked only by the ever-vigilant hustlers, operating solely with impunity.

b.h. shepherd. (23, austin, texas, usa)

quarter passed

kiss. by chloe lewis. (27, vancouver, british columbia, canada)

shining knight

by phil grooman

Shining bright he hears a call,
A song of beauty's soft white skin;
That skips upon the gentle breeze
With whispers of forgotten sin.

And shining bright he knows of death,
Of passage through that wooded cell;
That twists and turns in endless search
For spirit lost within the shell.

So shining bright he treads a path,
That ends upon a branch on high;
And there he finds seduction's voice
A-calling out her mournful cry.

Still shining bright he draws her close,
Embracing danger as a shroud;
And on that stream he floats away
To mornings buried deep in cloud.

And now he hides from shining brights,
The dawn sun burning glistened holes;
In dreams and hopes of foreign lands
Far oft from fallen forests souls.
And so he walks by candle bright,
Towards the lake of yesterdays;

quarter passed

And there he watches from the dark
His image dancing on the haze.

Shining bright in pale moon light,
The figure walks towards the shore;
Aloft his head he holds a sword
That burns the shapes of mortal scores.

It shines so bright that shadows flee,
And secrets carved in bark revealed;
Arise from death my broken child
Your fated path is not yet sealed.

Back shining bright he turns his face,
Towards the golden midday sun,
And there upon a ray of light
A lover's song has just begun.

◆◆◆

phil groman. (23, beijing, china)

light and darkness. by donia lilly. (28, pythagorio, samos, greece)

quarter passed

gay... in a good way
by jayar pacifico

His name is Alex. Alejandro, to be exact. Alexander, if you want to be American about it. I met him through a mutual friend and I knew he was gay by a nudge. Gay guys are all pretty much the same, horny as hell. Actually, that statement can apply to the world's entire male population. Statisticians apparently calculated that men think about sex every eight seconds. To me, that is an underestimation. Should be every five seconds; especially for those that haven't had it in a long time. Me, being one.

I met him once before at a club, which is the perfect place to flirt. No real talking going on unless you're yelling at each other so it's your body language that gets tested. Plus, the lighting will flatter any figure since the details are blanketed by shadows and alcohol. Our introduction was short and our conversation was even shorter. A set of glances were noticed but purposely not recognized. I think I actually avoided eye contact with him the whole night.

The art of eye contact can be tricky. There's a delicate balance to it. You don't want to stare at the floor while talking to someone nor do you want to stare at him. Staring is plain creepy, but looking away shows disinterest. Even if you're just a ball of nervous energy, not looking at someone is a complete turn off. I guess the key is to not tip the scales.

Months later, I saw him again at a mutual friend's party. I thought to myself that it must be fate. I wasn't sure what to make of the whole situation, not sure if he felt my eyes undressing him, wasn't sure if he was even remotely interested. But I was destined to talk to this guy, hook up with him, maybe pick at his brain. I didn't get to do the latter as much as I would have liked but at least I got two out of three. Can't win them all, right?

gay... in a good way

We started with a few casual conversations. Maybe some quiet, uncomfortable moments, too, but that's to be expected. Talking to a complete stranger sort of feels like a job interview. No one likes to be interviewed, but how else do you get to know someone? So, I started with the basics. I found out his age and his last name. I asked where he grew up, what he wanted to be when he grew up. He told me how many children he'd like to raise. Apparently, enough to field a whole football team. I asked questions about his family situation and how they reacted to the word "gay." How he came out and when.

I found out he's a gamer, likes role-playing, multi-player video games. I forgot the name of the game but he was on level twenty-nine at the time. Pretty sure it's different by now. And, since he didn't own a car, I was told he'd rather walk to work everyday rather than asking someone for a ride. His job was not close to home, at least a couple of miles away. This little factoid amazed me. It showed me what he went through on a daily basis, like he was stuck on survival. It made me want to take care of him. Hold him, sometimes.

I, on the other hand, was just bragging. Of course I didn't realize it at the time, but in retrospect, I was trying to sell myself to him like a used car salesmen with a combover. Shit, I should have just handed him my fucking resume. Given him a formal objective.

OBJECTIVE: To obtain a gay friendship, possibly a gay relationship, at least some lovin' for a night.

I thought I needed to pitch my qualities, my successes, my blessed life in order to show him what I can offer. I wanted his interest and had to appear as this great catch. But, my attempts failed because no one likes a bragger; it's a total turn off. I made myself out to be a two foot salmon worthy of picture taking (or a six foot marlin if you're the deep sea fishing type), only to realize later that I'm a horrible catch, a minnow. Technically, I'm what they use to catch "the catch." I'm bait. That sucks.

Through all that nonsense, he was kind enough to meet me after, say, the fifth phone call. We agreed on that Friday night, around 8ish, his place. Maybe

quarter passed

watch a scary movie, maybe some dinner, a bowl of ice cream, but it didn't turn out that way at all. It eventually became a "come over to my house and let's smoke up" situation.

Yes. It's what I wanted from the whole thing. I felt like an overfilled balloon at the highest volume capacity just ready to be popped. Or inhaled, if you're into the whole nitrous thing. Or helium, for the elementary minds. In all honesty, it had been a long time since I was intimate with someone, let alone a guy. My statistical frequency at that point was every two seconds. Sex. Would you like to get some drinks? Sex. How was your day? Sex. What time is it? Sex. The cycle is distracting.

I was excited but extremely nervous because I was never a confident person in bed. My ambivalence originally stemmed from what some call the "Asian curse." In simpler (and funnier) terms, it's a small penis. I suffer from small penis syndrome. People see it as low self-esteem, others see it as self-consciousness, self-awareness. Call it what you want; it's SPS to me. Most Asian countries are still searching for a cure. China recently invested a couple million to help the cause. A black ribbon is worn to show support. Oh, the irony.

In high school, I first learned that women aren't completely lying when they say size doesn't matter. That is, as long as you up the ante with skill. You know, the "motion of the ocean." My family is named after an ocean, thank you very much. Now, women are one thing, but with the stereotypes in my head, backed up by hours of watching gay porn, I concluded that gay men have a whole different set of standards. To them, I had gathered, bigger was always better.

Regardless of my shortcomings (pun intended), Friday finally arrived and I spent the day running errands with my daughter in the rear view mirror. I rushed from place to place to get things in order. When we stopped at McDonald's for lunch, I found the perfect opportunity to reflect on the past while considering my near future…

It was hard - still is - associating with homosexuality. I grew up in a Catholic home and was taught at a pretty young age that I was basically going to hell. I used to cringe at the word "gay," avoided it at all costs. It was one of the words brightly printed on the shirts inside the closet I called home for twenty-four years, along with fear, sin, rejection, shame, judgment, and porn, to name a few. They were constant reminders that I never had anything nice to wear. I'd come out every so often to dance or smoke a cigarette, but my heart would race every time I reached for that door knob. I always felt like some timer was set as I exited which increased my blood pressure and stimulated the sebaceous glands. Fight or flight always ended with flight for me. It was homophobia, fear of myself. I had midnight deadlines and three simple letters, G-A-Y, controlled my life.

When I was younger, I would always crush on the un-gettable girls. The ones who were perfect in every way. It wasn't a conscious thought but I eventually realized that liking these types of girls would prevent me from ever having to go down. They were decoys, functional. These girls were the perfectly spaced hangers in my color coordinated closet. Then I grew taller, smarter, and more attractive and suddenly, the un-gettable became gettable. They started to like me first. Fuck.

So, at seventeen, I gave it a try and lost my virginity to my chemistry tutor, Kirsten. Her intelligence and laid back attitude made her so sexy. Not to mention, she was the token white chick all Asian men fear. She was so amazing about making me feel comfortable and adequate. Reassured me that I always did a mighty fine job with her elusive orgasm. And, I discovered the warmth of the pussy. Man, it's like waking up under a thick down blanket on a cold Tahoe morning warm. So, pussy and I began having a public love affair. But, I was already privately in love with the penis.

Pretending to study the periodic table of elements but actually studying the effect of periodic clitoral stimulation, my parents caught us in my room one night. After the initial shock and disbelief from all parties involved, my mom looked disappointed, called me to her room and went on her usual, "How dare you disrespect this house?" lecture, beginning with, "Let's pray the Hail Mary to get you through the gates of Heaven." Meanwhile, my dad stood behind her occasionally making funny faces at me.

My quiet, well-mannered father was acting like a proud older brother as

quarter passed

his wife tried to discipline their son about the ramifications of premarital sex. What the hell? I couldn't help but laugh, which fueled my mom even more, adding two "Our Fathers" at the end. I'm sure he was just glad that his youngest son was not gay. Man, if he only knew.

I walked through college, too, as a heterosexual. By then, I had golf clubs and a refrigerator full of beer. They were eventually replaced with diapers, pacifiers and a diamond ring. My good judgment lapsed one night as I danced with alcohol and bong hits and my ex-girlfriend. We had unprotected sex, which led to nine months of utter fear, a reluctant engagement, and a lifelong companion, the love of my life, weighing in at seven pounds and eight ounces. It was the greatest day of my life. I watched my daughter's birth and polished a dull respect for all mothers, including my own, but I suddenly felt full assimilation into this heterosexual world.

Each day my personal space got smaller and smaller. Baby things are not that small, considering how tiny infants are as they exit the womb. I barely had room to move because the ball got heavier and the chain started to chafe. I could not breathe. I needed fresh, clean mountain air so I closed my eyes, braced myself and swung the closet door wide open for all to see. They were scared to peek in, expecting formaldehyde preserved severed heads and leather gloves, but all they found were bags of skittles and a dirty Rainbow Brite doll. With an engagement breached, a beautiful baby girl with my last name, a few tears in my eyes, I announced to the world that I needed to "find" myself.

And, there I was still lost and still searching while I finished off my daughter's chicken nuggets. As I recall, I heard her hum "Amazing Grace" at one point during a conversation. I thought to myself, "What the hell am I doing? I can't do this." So, I called him with the intention of cancelling. Two seconds later, I confirmed, then laughed at how quickly I had flipped. Sex.

I got ready like a teenage girl. Took a while in front of the mirror, popping my zits, wondering what he'll think of me, my skin. I never really had a problem with my skin, aside from the occasional bouts with adolescent acne. Once, I saw a documentary on TLC that tried to define beauty: wide nose, big ass, thin lips, giraffe necks. Qualities found unattractive in one region of the world were praised in another. Interesting, I thought. However, the show ended with this statement: the universal definition of beauty is good skin.

I got a big zit right on my nose the next day and they never stopped coming. Across the board, I was officially ugly. I created this vain fear which manifested into my reality. Now, I'm not even comfortable looking at myself in the mirror. How sad.

I was an honor roll student in high school, received numerous scholarships at graduation, managed a staff of projectionists at twenty-one years old, made $60,000 a year as a microbiologist when I was twenty-three, became a father at twenty-five, finished my first novel by twenty-six, and entered nursing school at twenty-seven. I had a large group of friends that respected and confided in me. I had a bond with my family that continued to strengthen on a daily basis. But, I would've traded it all to be well-endowed, with a nice complexion. To me, there was - and is - still no greater success in life than finding comfort in my naked body. I always admired the strippers, the streakers, the skinny dippers and the porn stars. I wanted the success they had. I would've signed on the dotted line as the devil smiled upon me. It was the truth and it fucking hurt.

Wishful thinking, I thought, as I popped the last juicy one. Then, I guess-timated how big Alex was, based on his size and frame, and hoped he wasn't doing the same to me. I took a shower and scrubbed a little harder. I shampooed twice while I mentally sifted through my wardrobe and figured what I was going to wear. I thought about my clean underwear and which would be the most attractive. I'm telling you… a girl.

Funny thing is, I tried to play dumb and act like it was still an innocent invite. That is, until I bought some alcohol. I walked out of the grocery store with liquid courage in hand and did a mental check:

Shower. Check.

Hair. Check.

Clean underwear. Check.

Breath mints. Check. Sex.

Cigarettes. Check.

quarter passed

Alcohol. Check.
Condoms. Check.
Okay. Ready.

"Hey Alex, I'm outside right now. Which house is it again? On the left or the right?"
"Don't worry, I'll come out."
"Cool."

The night was clear, a reassuring chill in the wind, a few stars were out. I walked toward him and I didn't know what to expect. Was I gonna give him a high five? A half shake, half hug? A full on hug? A kiss? No, not a kiss. Hell no, that would be too gay. What the hell is too gay? Either way, he came out and greeted me. I was feeling pretty uncomfortable and he saw it in my face. Was this going to be a wham-bam-thank-you-sir situation? I didn't know what to expect. Expect the worst and hope for the best. That's what you're supposed to do, right? We hugged.

We went into his house and this mini-party got going. I was introduced to his roommate, Kevin, who I recognized as an old friend's boyfriend. He was there to smoke up too. I wondered if he was gay. We got to talking. All a bunch of small talk; little, insignificant banter. Kevin started to pack the bowls and pass the bong around. I brought Sierra Nevada, a pale ale, and some flavored rum to drink. It was the worst combination ever. A shot of sweet, flavored rum followed by the bland, acquired taste of beer. Add cotton mouth to the equation and this whole scenario was completely not gay.

We talked about video games and talked about video games and talked about video games a little more. I don't play video games - was never strong on hand-eye coordination - so I just laughed along and asked questions as if I cared. Then we talked about school and smoking weed and drinking and mutual friends. I was sure that this was a recipe for disappointment. I sat there talking to Kevin and not even looking at Alex. Where was that fucking scale? And right when the thought came to mind, in walked my old friend, Sammi, whom I hadn't seen in years. Another delay. Fuck.

gay... in a good way

It had been a while since we last talked and I'd forgotten that she's a gabber. She's intelligent with a lot of interesting things to say - real substance to her words - but I was not feeling it that night. I was tired of talking of the past, our youth, our mistakes and I just wanted to taste his lips. After Sammi finally finished making her three-hour-long point, we rushed off to his room.

Sex. The. Sex. balloon. Sex. was. Sex. way. Sex. beyond. Sex. inflated. Sex. and. Sex. a. Sex. pin. Sex. was. Sex. an. Sex. inch. Sex. away. Sex. from. Sex. contact. Sex. Actually, it had popped already, about twenty minutes ago.

Walking into his room was like walking into the unknown. I expected it to be pink or something. But, it wasn't. It was a normal room with Mr. Marley nicely idolized. It had a bed and a closet, of course. The essentials. Once the door was closed, I remember immediately kissing him. I wanted him so bad and I thought, I hoped, actually I knew the feelings were mutual. He wanted it too.

Finally. My tension was released and good God almighty, was it released. As if I inhaled that nitrous-filled balloon in one shot. I basically got five years of homosexual sexual tension off my back. I felt like I could breathe again while I kissed this man. A beautiful, strong, brave, intelligent, young man. I kissed him with so much force, so much sadness that I lost myself. I got lost in this course of confused thought and as much as I try,

I can only remember a few brief moments in full detail. But, the ones that I do remember are so clear and vivid. Mostly the kissing. I felt like I had to show him how it was done, but he caught on real fast - eventually, teaching me. When I told him of my insecurity with my skin, he kissed it. He kissed my thorns and made me feel so beautiful and desired. I had porcelain smooth skin at that very moment. Yes, it was that good.

Then came the disrobing. Boy, was I pleasantly surprised. And, as expected, he was pleasantly disappointed (played off as excited). I was lying down and he immediately got on top of me. I could feel his body close to mine. His neck was long. His energy was warm. We were both beautiful. He was naked and perfect while I still had my shirt on. It never came off.

I remember the moment of contact. Parts of my body I didn't think could feel

quarter passed

were suddenly stimulated, even my fingernails had a heart beat. I remember looking down and seeing this small framed man completely satisfying me. He got my blood flowing after we found the rhythm between us, setting off a storm of endorphins that charged like never before. Attack, attack. Pleasurable pain. Couldn't feel the effects of the alcohol or weed anymore.

It took me a while to catch up to him. It wasn't 'til the act was completely over when I finally did. This was my epiphany. It was gay sex. It was good sex. It was the right kind of sex. But, I was shaking in pure sadness. I was soaking in my own sweat and gathering my guilt. It was the moment when I came to the conclusion that I must be gay.

Fuck.

I was struck with this urge to leave. Tick, tock, tick. It was unsettling. I was afraid he'd decide that he had made a mistake or I would finally realize that I made the mistake. My mind was burning. I felt scattered as he lay completely still and completely sexy. He was so ideal in this pose.

I went to use the bathroom and wanted to get a drink of water. I hoped he would come with me so we could laugh at what just happened. We could make a joke of it and sort of ease back into heterosexuality. But, he was knocked out. Typical guy, I thought. That "roll over and sleep" act is blind to sexual orientation. All men do it.

Beyond the immediate guilt, I walked back to the room feeling pretty happy. I saw this exhausted young man and assumed I did a good job. I gave myself a figurative high five, did a little dance. Tired that fucker out. I glanced for the last look as I left and I noticed the slight smile on his face. I still have a mental picture of that smile - a smile of satisfaction, thank you very much.

I, too, had a smile. But mine lasted for a while. I was dazed. I floated. At the time, I honestly didn't think I was going to ever see this guy again so I wanted to enjoy it for as long as possible. I wanted to wrap the moment up in a box, like a small present to myself, and to find it years later; to remember the tune of the night. I couldn't stop thinking about him, so I called the next day to confess my thanks. A very well-received thank you.

About a week or so later, we decided to hang out, just two normal friends with nothing great intended. But, I learned something new about him. He loved Christmas lights. Christmas decorations, in general. Sex. It was cold that night and he asked if I wanted to go to the tree lighting ceremony in town. I had never been to one before so I got excited. I thought it was cute and romantic and festive. We got to the lighting and there was nothing spectacular. It was actually over with just a couple of people lingering. We saw the tree and I was disappointed because the lights were a bit too purple for my gay taste. It's kind of funny when you think about it - purple. Who uses purple lights on a Christmas tree? Just seemed wrong.

Unsatisfied, we went to a neighboring city to compare its tree. A little better, but not by much. At least it wasn't purple, I thought. After grabbing some coffee, we walked to a nearby park and he took me down a long flight of stairs with a creek running by us. We were alone. Alone and cold. We huddled near each other to keep warm. I should have taken that moment to kiss him but I was afraid of being seen. Gay and exposed. No way. Sure, they would have been strangers that saw us but public display of affection is just not my style. Either way, it was a romantic spot with a pretty romantic guy.

That was the best or possibly the worst thing that happened. I started to get all giddy thinking about him. My hormones were raging and I wanted more. I wanted to experience it again. But, it never happened again. I think - actually, I'm pretty confident - that I scared him off. I began to call like there was no time to waste. Flight, flight. I wanted to see him so badly, even in my dreams. But he was not feeling it like I had assumed in the beginning.

Truth is, I wasn't his type. He made that clear. We were two completely different people. Different interests, different upbringings, different stages in life with the same sexual orientation. I realized that I was searching for a relationship, a gay one. And, that was the only criteria that needed to be met. All you had to be was a man and gay. With Alex, these criteria were met and I wanted to fly with him.

I wanted to take him by the hand and say, "Come with me; I'll show you a life of happiness." However, the road blocks were placed, maybe a couple of DUI checkpoints, a few hidden cops waiting to stop us; but it was Alex who placed them

quarter passed

there. He was the one that didn't want to go with me and I understand why now.

I have self-esteem issues, phobias, overwhelming insecurities. I often bring people down with me. A paranoid thought is just like acne. Just don't know when or where either is going to show up. It's hard to deal with and way beyond my conscious control sometimes. I accused him of using me. How might this come about, you ask, when it was me that flaunted my money in his face, wanting to treat him to everything we did? Wasn't it me who talked finances more than him? Yes. Wasn't it me who talked about careers and education and success? Yes.

I laid the concrete to be stepped on. I was basically wearing a sign around my neck. Actually, it was a large tattoo on my forehead in bold font that said "USE ME!" It's hard to admit, but my resume was falsified.

Surprisingly enough, he overlooked my posturing and gave me another chance. No strings attached, purely platonic. A friendship that humbled me and helped me realize that the gay stereotypes in my head are only kept alive by people like me - the ignorant, phobic kind. A friendship that showed me how to finally turn off that fucking timer and take things a little slower. Sex. I didn't have many gay friends - at least none that I could watch scary movies with - but now I had Alex. It took some time but I eventually realized he wasn't my type either.

Alex may be younger, he may be smaller but he's the better person, has the bigger heart, and the bigger - well, you know. And he's wiser, beyond my years. I thank him. I care about him. He was comfortable in his own skin, never hid in a closet, and worked his ass off for his very own car.

It's good to know that I'll still have my little present to open every now and then. I'll listen to the tune with admiration and reflect on the memory with warm, fuzzy feelings. I just hope he'll occasionally open his up, watch the ballerina spin and close it right when the music chimes, "… was blind but now I see." Hopefully, he'll even take quiet pleasure in knowing that he helped me somehow. I wouldn't mind at all.

After the years have come and gone, maybe we won't be that great of friends. Maybe we'll slowly weed the thoughts of each other out of our minds. Maybe he hasn't given us a thought since that night. But one thing is for sure: If I ever, EVER come across anything remotely resembling a large, purple-lit Christmas tree,

gay... in a good way

I will always think of him. Really. A purple Christmas tree? Come on now, that's just gay - in a bad way, as he would say.

◆◆◆

jayar pacifico. (29, fairfield, california, usa)

quarter passed

crystal raindrop. by karishma singh. (22, mumbai, india)

deactivated ballad

by owen austin

she calls me out
with her softest whisper
out of the leaves -
a sad, oily dog
that couldn't catch a meal.
reaching into my heart, silent,
with her limbs.
in me
love has been deactivated.
by some bastard I can't name anymore
with various faces.
I can't blame my father, my mother
my friends or lovers.
not even the kids that shoved my face
into the water fountain
in ninth grade.
and I'm looking through the glass
of a right side up reality
cuz it is just what it is.
so what's this now.
who is she, calling me out.
stormy long eyes
warm dark skin
calling me out.

owen austin. (28, tokyo, japan)

quarter passed

domestic discipline
by maria gregoriou

Here's to her.
She managed it at last,
to poke and push you
Into a corner,
Hold you down long enough
to extract that wild flair
You held onto with all your spirit.
So now you are tamed,
broken into loyalty.
She cut and trimmed away
all the verging roughness,
Shaped a cardboard uniform
and pinned it on the stiff
silhouette of what you used to be,
when you once excelled
In the unaccepted.
But how can you constrain the fierce
to meek and call it beautiful?
I break my thirst in her name.

maria gregoriou. (28, nicosia, cyprus)

shelley croatia. by tim martin. (26, london, england)

quarter passed

the red dress in the window
by amy bleu

Red dress in the window
Keeps me wanting
In a life so full and blessed
It is only materials
Like a dress that leaves me unrequited
No, I don't believe a dress
Could need me, too
And I could never be faithful –
How could I wear one dress for life?
Let's have a brief affair
Then I could wear you, out
But never wear you out
Feel your power for one great night
Your red, merlot
Low-cut, "Monroe"
Are you silk, satin, or chiffon?
I may never know, for I cannot bear
To look upon your price tag
But I am certain: you're worth a fortune.

◆◆◆

amy bleu. (25, portland, oregon, usa)

mixing up

by daniel davy

The wheezing turd was right. Allie did look like a boy. Over an Incubus t-shirt, she wore jean overalls that extended down to her ankles, revealing red-white-red Cat In The Hat socks. A black barbell pierced her left eyebrow, and a blue glint studded her right nostril. Her shoulders were wider than mine, and a blonde ridge of a fauxhawk bisected her Army buzzcut. She had a Japanime Tinkerbell nose that scimitared away from her cherubic cheeks, and she smelled like Camel cigarettes and hand sanitizer. But, she wasn't bowed by the wheezing turd's attempt to rile her.

Before I could chastise the obese and very violent teen, Allie responded, "I get that a lot. Doesn't bother me."

A simple, perfectly disarming response. This girl has no fear, I thought. It was day one in Baobab Cottage, a lock-down facility for depressive and assaultive kids in extreme crisis, and she had no fear. Was she aware that our adolescent "clients" knowingly spit STD's daddy gave them into our eyes (thank god for goggles)? That they shatter their favorite Insane Clown Posse CD and rake the opalescent shards over already scarred wrists to exercise the first self-control of their lives. That, unprovoked, they lunge hyena-like with their teeth flashing at your crotch before being dragged by four latex-gloved staff to the Quiet Room.

Maybe her voice would've wavered a little more if she'd known that this wheezing turd, this peachfuzz Humpty Dumpty, had smuggled six razor blades (taped to his thighs) into the Cottage and distributed them to the Cutters and some of our more psychotic clients. Several seasoned staff quit upon hearing about this "Razorblade Brigade." Did she know, or not? Either way, I was impressed. But Allie wasn't my type.

I never did the counter-culture thing; no tattoos, no piercings, no dra-

quarter passed

matic fashion statements, no heavy drugs. I was content in my skin, the product of intelligent, nurturing, dedicated parents and was never gnawed by transformative teenage angst or any of the other catalysts that compel youths to markedly alter their raw identities. My tastes were thusly monochromatic and shaded by the not-too-ambitious desire for a fun, attractive girlfriend. So at the Gemini Bar after work when our beery co-workers began wedging their elbows between my ribs, wagging their heads towards Allie, I was initially uninterested. I cited a lack of attraction.

"Never been into short hair or overalls." I declared my distaste for smokers.

But Allie dogged me to play pool every night after work, and I've never been able to resist a game of pool. Something woven deeply into the thin felt, something about the elusive spins, the stripe-solid constellations, the extreme geometrical focus has always fascinated me. Nightly, armed with an Alaskan Amber or a Bridgeport Ale, we weighed our cue sticks and shoved three quarters along with the day's manifold stresses into the dormant table. We peered at one another like snipers over polished shafts tipped in chalk until we found the shortest distance between two points.

Over the moss green expanse (her exact eye color) we flirted and fought. En-Garde. Wink, smile. Touché. Legs bent; knees spread; neck craned; elbows cocked; arms rubbing like polished stones underwater until the clacked black 8-Ball sinks into plastic shadows. I let her win a few games, and she knew it. She denounced my chivalry as "anachronistic and sexist" and refused to play again unless I promised to beat the crap out of her, if I could.

I quickly became addicted to our nightly billiard sessions - to Allie's charm and toughness - and our co-workers knew it. They snickered knowingly in the Gemini haze. Unembarrassed, I sank to my knees and begged for another game, vowing to strip Allie of any dignity she possessed, ball by vanishing ball. We soon evolved to challenging friends and bar-goers for beer and jukebox rights. The 8-Ball Gods blessed us without fail, and we quickly rose to fearsome-twosome status in the Gemini's admittedly miniscule pool circle.

On our first date, Allie stuffed daffodil pillows down my shirt. A friend had convinced me (pitcher after pitcher) to be a Polaroid Santa Claus for her kindergarten class' annual fundraiser. Allie heard the news through the crocheted grapevine that wound around every branch in Baobab Cottage. She proposed to share my ignominy as a sidekick elf. All St. Nick's need sidekick elves, she insisted, to judo-chop those misguided Pumpkin Kings that lurk like daddy-long-legs in kindergarten corners. What would happen to all those midget harbingers of disease, those trollish hopefuls, if their Santa Claus never arrived to chase momma-made gingersnaps with warm milk? I needed Allie and her elfin fists of fury if I was to survive this holiday do-goodery.

We stepped out of Allie's sleigh (VW Beetle) ten minutes before show time, and I was pitching a strong case to Guinness for Most Malnourished Santa of All-Time. Ever the resourceful elf, Allie scoured the tinsel bedecked classroom and emerged with six daffodil pillows (naptime accessories?) and two grubby rolls of toilet paper. She stuffed me like a turducken. We pasted on our smiles, took our positions in front of the camera, framed by candy canes fit for Gulliver, and the first teary, writhing victim was shoved into my lap.

A sallow boy without dimples, all ankles knees and elbows, bucks upwards epileptically on my lap. Lemur eyes caught in glittery cotton ball clouds on the ceiling. My rumpled left arm hooks around his stomach. Embroidered daffodils creep over a brass button into snowy beard threads. Allie in pool-felt elf garb. Red circles stippled on her cheeks. Dark runless tights funneling into curly-toed shoes. The only one looking at the camera.

Date 2: *Shaun of the Dead*. Date 3: Sushi and bowling. No kisses yet. Everything at a comfortable half-speed.

Date 4 was a 10 p.m. trip to Portland's manicured jewel, the Test Rose Garden, Allie's idea, an after-dinner whim. Her lashes caught the moonlight, dividing it into hundreds of eye-shadowed arcs. Her lips were thinly veiled in plum-purple. Her hair was a little longer, sans fauxhawk, a new color. She changed colors like a Nevada sunset after a nuclear test, like a chameleon wandering through a kaleidoscope. Fluorescent pink waves now whorled around her elfin ears. Her perfumed wrists had a scent of hushed secrets, like Egypt, like a chocolate yawn. I smelled like bad cough drops, like an emergency room. I had a phlegmy cough all week and,

quarter passed

worrying that a Robitussin hint (sterile cherry-flavored) might escape my mouth, I treated myself to Tic-Tacs aplenty and half-shots of Listerine.

High above the city blare, we ambled through the empty parking lot, shoulders pressed together as if we were front row in a Green Day concert. Conjoined by a vague heat no sleeves, jean or otherwise, could contain. At the garden entrance (brick arch through a hedge) we were confronted by a rusting sign hanging from rotting wooden posts. An old sentinel guarding the Garden at the behest of paranoid, floraphile fogies. It was the only recipient of light in the encroaching mist, a gluey, yellow beam anchored in dying grass and was surrounded by pinwheeling brushstrokes. A pointillist profusion of immodest pinks, lascivious reds, bold purples. All gyrating in a dark olive-green sea like pool balls spun oven a sinister table. The sign was hopelessly out of place. A sweaty sock pressed into a burnished silver picture frame encrusted with rubies and pink sapphires. In militant letters it frowned:

MANY ROSES ARE PROTECTED UNDER COMMERCIAL PATENT RIGHTS. THERE IS A PORTLAND CITY ORDINANCE SPECIFYING A $500 FINE FOR THE UNAUTHORIZED REMOVAL OF ROSES FROM THE GARDEN.

Protected. Unauthorized. We shivered in the encircling fog. Anticipation condensed on our eyelids. How could we resist? We took turns being lookout and plucker. The stems were fibrous, like bamboo, and the thorns elicited more than a Disney drop of blood from misplaced fingers. While Allie was on the lookout, I wrapped my fingers as best I could around the stem of a rose tinged blue in the haze. Burgundy Iceberg. I twisted and ripped the stubborn plant until it finally severed, its stem reduced to tough ribbons flecked with blood. I wiped my hands and hid it under my jean jacket where it pricked my ribs slightly at every step. Waiting for an opportune moment, I walked towards Allie, shrugged my shoulders, and suggested we wave a white flag or, in our case, a latex glove I had pocketed during the day at Baobab Cottage. Our surrender to the roses finalized, we sat on a concrete bench with a city view.

Allie was sucking on butterscotch. I had snuck a peppermint while she was

mixing up

on lookout. A security guard swept his flashlight over the roses in a garden tier beneath us. He whistled Otis Redding's "Sitting on the Dock of the Bay." A harsh cough forced my lips apart before I could suppress it. Allie rubbed my back in shapes like we do for the ADHD kids at work. It grounds them, reconfigures their cross-wired senses. Works with autism too.

What shape is this? Now this? A slow triangle, a trapezoid, a tiny octagon. And then spirals upon spirals. Her fingers spelunked the knobs of my spine and traced my shoulder blades creating more shapes on the canvas of my back, geometrically guiding me towards her until we were face to face. Pool-felt irises spoked with jade. Again I coughed a sterile peppermint burst.

"You don't mind that I'm sick?"

She leaned in pressing against the thorns beneath my jacket. Ribs, thorns, ribs. I couldn't even move to present her with the bloody Burgundy Iceberg. Mesmerized in the haze, vine-like, she crept her fingers from my shoulder and wove them into mine. The peripheral shapes disappeared and with them my anchor to the garden, to the city, to my mind. My face was shrouded in electric pink. A slight opening. Slowly a butterscotch spoon dipped in peppermint syrup. Sliding, slipping. Again and again. The mixing of mysteries. The mixing-up of histories. Sliding, slipping…

who the fuck am I
who the fuck am
who the fuck
who the
who?

◆◆◆

daniel davy. (24, san rafael, california, usa)

quarter passed

lovers. by gina dunn. (26, dallas, texas, usa)

5

loss and challenge

simon

by maya bastian

I once ran into him at a party. The sort of one night, balls-out bender that you attended back when you were invincible. A drug-addled daze where his voice appeared out of the darkness – broad smile, structured jaw. My friend Simon gently cupped my face in his hands, staring at me as though he were the proudest of fathers.

"Maya, you vision, you beauty, you pure woman, you."

With such integrity and gusto, he belts out a line that I have been waiting to hear my whole life. Then he disappears into the girth of my ego, and we return to the night that we came here to enjoy.

In that brief moment, I remember thinking how much he looked like a politician. Not a Richard Nixon/George Bush, shifty-eyed, dishonest crossbreed, but more like a real politician. You know, back in the old days when there seemed to be men of honor. Men you trusted to save your country from the whims of evildoers. Abe Lincoln. Andrew Jackson.

My friend Simon looks like that, with a long, thin face, bearded and likeable; rosy cheeks with a firm handshake; and bright, sparkling eyes, as though he knows things about you that even you don't know. I told him later that if he ever decided to run for president, he would have my vote.

He just laughed and asked, "President of what?"

He's the kind of guy with whom you can sit and converse for hours about anything and everything. A broad scope of knowledge, yet he always maintains the infinite grace of humility. Rarely have I seen him compete for attention with his knowledge, which is so often the case among the intelligent. Instead, he sits quietly, listening, reflecting and awaiting his turn. From this perspective, he seems a champion among men.

quarter passed

On the day I return for my second visit at his bedside, I am late. The ward is still, yet far from peaceful. I worry that visiting hours are coming to a close, and I have yet to find my friend. I'm not sure what to expect when I get there; however, I'm fairly certain that he will be in good spirits. This is a guy who never fumbles around in the dark when there is a light nearby. This is a guy who dressed up as a munchkin on Halloween and somehow managed to pull it off with charm and panache. No shame. No fuss. Not a thing to worry about.

After a few wrong turns, I finally enter the room he is sharing with three older gentlemen who look withered with pain. My heart skips a beat. I hear a familiar voice and immediately recognize Simon's girlfriend. She is on the phone. I turn the corner and he looks up, startled.

For a brief moment I see something that I cannot place in his eyes. He is waiting for something, an answer, a calling. It's almost as if he was anticipating one of two visitors; a doctor or Death.

When he realizes it's me, his eyes well up and he looks away calling out that he wants to go home, please somebody let him go home. I feel useless and awkward at first, glancing over at his girlfriend to shoulder the burden. But she is distracted and doesn't look up.

Then something takes over within me, this mothering, nurturing force so complete, so feminine that I rush to his bedside and cover his face with kisses and hold him while he sobs and sobs and sobs. I don't let go. I feel his suffering as though it were my own. I open my heart up and let it overwhelm me in a misguided effort to relieve him. I want so desperately to heal him, to free him, an emotion that I have never discovered before this. In this moment, I give to him as much of myself as there is to give.

And then he falls asleep. Something, I am told, he has not been able to do since he was diagnosed one week earlier.

In that instant, I felt the depths of a boy that I never really knew before. His vulnerability allowed me to see him for who he really was in that brief moment: scared and alone, fighting a losing battle against Nature, God and himself. It felt innate to want to give of myself, to come to his aid. And so I did. Yet it was not enough.

simon

It is not the death or the dying that frightens me. Not the loss or the grief. It is the suffering. The dismal separation of self and universe where we fully realize how fragile humanity is. How fragile I am. And I have no super powers, no über-human strength to fight and win this futile battle. It continues within me and without me.

I feel as though I have righteously and officially been put in my place.

❖❖❖

maya bastian. (27, toronto, ontario, canada)

quarter passed

walk the line. by jessica darmanin. (21, woodbridge, ontario, canada)

smile, buddy
by maria giuliani

(Dedication to a Forgotten Face)

Walking along, all alone
My head faced down, blocking out the passers-by
Who threaten to interrupt my thoughts
Or threaten to interpret them
And I see it, a penny on the ground

My mind full of questions
Frustrations overflowing at the answers that don't come
And as I brew a half-pot of unhappiness
A random voice calls "smile, buddy"
A random voice, a forgotten face

Unsure of my surroundings
Not knowing how
Forgetting to learn
Insecure in the darkness of my shadow
Somewhere a little boy hops along singing,
"I did so many things I didn't know I could do today"

And I remind myself to think small
Look beyond the despair, the answer is there
Because the truth is not that I am alone
The truth is that I have an attitude problem
"Whatever" is so passive-aggressive

quarter passed

Synonymous with "unwilling to see"
Unhappiness more potent than acknowledging potential
Not doing safer than doing
Living was easier without a child's wonderment
But I was sinning against myself

And years went by without laughing
Months went by unowned
Hours pulled and gouged and made me invisible to myself
About to witness the underside of a rock

But I saw butterflies, bees and pregnant ladies
An outstretched hand meant for giving, not taking
And I remembered that the answer is there
Beyond the despair
And now because my vocabulary exists in only two words
To that outstretched hand I voice "Thank you"

◆◆◆

maria giuliani. (26, montreal, quebec, canada)

despair. by mike foster. (25, fort lauderdale, florida, usa)

stupidest thing i've ever done

by sharyn goldyn

We all do stupid shit when we're young. No. Forget that. Young or old, we all, as a human race, do stupid shit. But I must admit that by far the dumbest thing I have ever done was moving into a crack house when I was twenty.

It wasn't like I answered an ad that said, "*Crack house looking for tenant.*" It was more like, "*Two artists – one a DJ and guitarist, the other a young painter – looking for an artistic, like-minded roommate.*" And then, to add icing to the cake: "*Shared car and beautiful flat.*" It was a wonderful, simple ad that made me forget all the other apartments I had lined up to visit and instantly choose that one, no further research needed.

A few days after I read the ad, I met Bryn, a beautiful young redhead, and Khaled (Kay-led), a fat two-braided Egyptian with terrible, terrible skin. Bryn was the painter (though she only had one painting that I, to this day, have ever seen – and it was unfinished) and Khaled was the DJ/guitarist willing to share his junky car.

Though I am known for my poor character judgment, both seemed like "cool, quality" people so I moved into the apartment without much questioning and paid Khaled a $1250 cash deposit. Only then did I find out that Khaled did a little bit of mixing – cocaine. That is, on our stove. And sure, he did play guitar, but only wrist-slitting Elliott Smith covers and only between bong hits, which were scheduled about every five minutes.

I was at a complete loss as to what to do when I moved in with someone whose entire existence, at this point, revolved around drugs. I stayed in the apartment for a couple of agonizing, "*Requiem for a Dream*"-type weeks before I summoned enough money to put down a deposit on a new place and pay another month's rent.

stupidest thing i've ever done

This left me free from the waves of second-hand crack smoke, but completely and utterly shit broke, too.

There was one small hope that I wouldn't be broke for long since (theoretically) I would be getting my large deposit back from Khaled, but the possibility shrank at an alarming rate (along with my bank account balance) when Khaled refused to return my calls.

It had been about three weeks since me and Bryn had moved out of the crack house when I decided that yet another call to Khaled was needed. I didn't want to bother or fuck with a crackhead but he did, after all, owe us each $1250, which I stupidly had no tangible proof of. And though I knew he didn't have the cash, I needed it.

I needed anything, five dollars, two hundred, fifty cents… Shit, did I need money. I had become an involuntary vegetarian, eating peanut butter and jelly, bananas and Fruit Loops for days straight. I had five inaccessible dollars in my bank account and not even enough loose change to ride the bus for $1.25. I became an avid green tea drinker and eventually gave in and drank it without honey, my favorite thing in the world. Even Kool-Aid had become an extravagance.

I was so broke and desperate that I nearly lost my dignity. Though I didn't ask anyone to borrow money (and nobody had any), I did have a constant urge to steal. I found stealing to be somewhat of an art. The trick was to pay for at least one item, while hiding the rest wherever possible. Fruit markets were the easiest. You could pay for a bag of apples, but have a sack of cherries, grapes, and oranges tucked away in your backpack. No one suspects you if you go up to the counter and pay for something, and even if they do suspect you, it's best to choose a fruit market where they don't speak English and accusations are beyond their vocabulary.

But there were times when fruit just didn't cut it and I was so hungry and desperate for something-not-fruit that I wanted to walk into any of the shops on my street and just be like, "Hey, nobody's around, can I get a free meal?" But that would, of course, make me officially a beggar.

One thing that made me both sad and grateful was realizing that I'm not alone in this situation and that most of us are living day-to-day, meal-to-meal,

quarter passed

paycheck-to-paycheck. Fucking ramen.

The only lesson I had decided to learn from my poverty (aside from don't move in with crackheads) was that there is a huge difference between being broke and living with your parents in a warm, furnished house and being broke on your own, wondering if that box of whatever in the corner of the pantry is edible. And those who had the luxury of their parent's money were looked down upon while my poverty was a reflection of good character and nobility. Unfortunately, being poor was the easiest way to make me feel like I'd been rejected from the human race.

At first I tried to be positive about my lack of resources. I was going to actually go ahead and be Buddhist. At least then I would have a more logical, spiritual reason to be hungry and not buy anything, shed all materialism. Problem is I'm a skinny girl and I love food and my body processes everything twice as fast as it's consumed so I live in a constant state of hypoglycemia. So I eventually said to myself, "Fuck Buddhism, I'm having a PB and J." Still, I knew I wasn't too bad off because I had a friend who was eating peanut butter and jelly with no bread.

Aside from mastering the art of appearing like I am doing nothing wrong when I am stealing, I came across a few other tricks to get by when life isn't giving me any help.

One is having a very large bag or purse. I could go to Subway and order the most pathetic sandwich and simply slip chips and a bottled drink into my bag while sandwich artists joked amongst themselves, paying no heed to me.

I mastered sneaking onto the bus, getting on at the busiest stops and stepping in when the middle door opened to let passengers off. I would cross my fingers and sweat a little, hoping the bus driver wouldn't call me out like I had seen done to many bums trying the same maneuver.

I learned that if the recycled clothing shop won't buy your clothes one day, you can go in the next day to a different seller and they will most likely buy the same clothes that had been turned down the day before.

I learned to buy hardcover books from the Salvation Army for a dollar and sell them back to used bookstores for four.

I learned which stops and which hours were best to bring out my violin and

stupidest thing i've ever done

play to earn money. (The most I ever made was sixty dollars in a forty-five minute span.)

But, in spite of my cleverness, I was still perpetually broke and saving a couple extra bucks by sneaking onto the bus or stealing a drink from Subway wasn't going to pay my landlord, Susannah, who had a habit of taping neat, little notes in fluorescent pink highlighter on my door saying, "Sharyn, this is serious, I need the rent." If only I had it, Suze.

Needless to say, the only way Susannah was going to get her rent was if Khaled, my Egyptian crackhead, gave me back the deposit.

I was on the phone waiting for Khaled to pick up when my new roommate Marc poked inside from the back door saying his job interview went well. Marc made me feel slightly better about my own position. He was fresh from Britain, the kind of guy who didn't buy drugs but managed to always be fucked up - a constant squatter - and more broke than me. He spooned the rice I was cooking on the stove and asked me if I was going to eat it.

He was perpetually "skint," stoned, and hungry. I always thought he was saying "skin." When we would ask him to pitch in money for beer or for a cab or for all our food he was eating he would say, "Naa, man, I'm skin."

I asked him once to spell it out loud and he said, "S-K-I-N-T." and I thought to myself, that should be the name of something: skint.

SKINT. I was fucking skint.

sharyn goldyn. (22, chicago, illinois, usa)

quarter passed

belgrade shanty. by frederick bernas. (20, london, england)

my life's education
by artila devi

When I was young, I was brought up with the notion that hard work and good grades would pay off - that they were all that one required to succeed in life. Parents, teachers and other figures of authority all asserted that the better my grades were, the better job I would get, the more chances of promotion I would have and the more secure my future would be. It made sense to me. I could see no reason why the diligent student would not turn out to be the successful professional.

Discovering my calling, however, was no easy feat. At first, I wanted to become a lawyer. My grandfather did not approve. Next, I thought of becoming a doctor. When I went to the hospital with my grandmother and saw a man being wheeled in on a stretcher, covered in blood, suddenly medicine no longer seemed attractive. For a time, no occupation seemed truly desirable. My career counselor nearly gave up on me, until I realized that I was a pretty good teacher.

As the eldest child in my family, I spent years tutoring my younger siblings and cousins. Being an educator became natural. When I announced my chosen vocation, everyone was pleased. My grandparents were impressed with the prospect of a good salary and a respectable profession, and my parents were happy that it would mean long holidays with them. Little did we know what the future held in store.

My professional journey began the day I visited the Ministry of Education to submit my application for the position of 'Teacher of English - Secondary School.' I had completed my degree and was looking forward to teaching at a local high school. I had no doubt in my mind that the Ministry would call me in for an interview or give me a posting within a few days.

quarter passed

For the next week, I waited in vain for a phone call, a letter, or any sign from the Ministry. One of my friends tried to convince me that I might have better luck turning up at the Ministry office in person. I could not grasp the logic behind her words. I thought, surely, the Ministry would review each application thoroughly and post teachers who merited a position. But with each passing day, my friend's words became more persuasive and, in spite of my skepticism, I eventually gave up waiting for the phone to ring and went to investigate the delay.

At the Ministry, I soon discovered, people came in as early as 6:00 am to be the first in line, spending whole days packed into the cramped office. Some were lucky and received placements. Others sat there day after day, waiting. As days, weeks and months passed and the new school term began, I remained unlucky and unemployed. Because I couldn't bear to sit at home and do nothing, my parents agreed to help finance my education further, assured that a higher degree would guarantee my spot in the workforce. I went back to the university to pursue postgraduate studies. Luckily, the faculty allowed me to do odd jobs for a few courses as well, and I started working as a part-time marker.

Shortly thereafter, it came to my attention that a new university had opened its doors. I applied for an open position and was thrilled when they offered me a full-time, three-year contract. I was finally going to start my long-awaited career. The only problem was that this new university was in another city, and my parents, with the events and violence of the 2000 coup still fresh in their minds, were concerned for my safety.

The name of my country, Fiji, is known across the world for two main reasons: First, for its lovely smiles, friendly people, beautiful beaches and great bargains. Second, four coups have taken place in a span of only twenty years.

I saw this job as a golden opportunity so, despite my parents' concerns, I moved to the other city to begin working. Six months after I took up my appointment, I was content and well on my way to establishing myself when my father fell ill. He fell so ill, in fact, that he had to resign from his job. My mom also had to resign her own work in order to look after him.

Suddenly, at twenty-two years of age, I was my family's sole breadwinner. I started shuttling back and forth between my hometown and my adopted workplace.

my life's education

My meager salary - the university had just opened its doors and could not afford to pay its pioneering staff well - was divided into three parts. The first third of my salary went towards bills and rent. Another third went home to my parents and my younger brother. The remainder was spent on groceries and commuting, and it quickly became difficult for me to make ends meet. To save money, I began switching off lights early, taking shorter showers and traveling on buses. But these incremental savings weren't large enough to offset my family's mounting needs.

I soon began looking for a job closer to home because my father, fearing that he did not have long to live, wanted me nearby. When the university near my parents posted an opening for a one-year position at double my current salary, I resigned from my post without much regret.

I moved back home, took the new job and, for a time, things improved. In November, a few weeks before my year-long contract was due to expire, the acting Head of School called me into her office and informed me that the faculty had to downsize, and the first cuts would be tutors. My contract would not be renewed. Jobless again, I went back to the Ministry of Education to ask to be absorbed into the high school system. Only, now, I was over-qualified!

So, I yet again sought refuge in part-time work. The faculty at the university and other area schools managed to give me a couple of hours of teaching and some marking. I took on four different courses to try and make due with what work I could get. Every day I would commute between campuses, picking up assignments to mark or returning the marked ones. Every night, I stayed up past midnight getting my work done.

The stack of bills at home prevented me from saving any money, and it quickly became a struggle to earn enough to support my entire family. I began feeling depressed and hopeless and my body kept telling me to slow down, but I had responsibilities that could not be neglected or delayed: shopping for food, paying for fuel, providing for my younger brother, and so on.

The strain of the work schedule and my emotional burden eventually took its toll on me and one day, while driving to drop off a batch of marked assignments, I feel asleep at the wheel. I hit another car and, although I luckily escaped the accident injury-free, both cars suffered substantial damage. My insurance company

quarter passed

proved to be unreliable in my hour of need, and I ended up having to repair both cars at my own cost - about $4,000 and two months' time.

At work, weeks passed before I finally received an offer for a six-month full time contract. I took the job without hesitation so, once again, I find myself at the beginning of the employment cycle. I have an office, but I haven't moved in any of my personal items or placed books on the shelves. After all, just how quickly will the next six months pass? Will I have some job security in six months or will I have to fall back on part-time work to get by?

My life has educated me in ways that a textbook never could. When I reflect upon my career to-date, I often question the value of getting good grades in school. My two degrees couldn't put food on the table, cure my sick father, or afford my family and me any security for our futures. I wish that someone had taught me when I was younger that life is uncertain and that nothing is guaranteed. This is wisdom that I can pass on - because I have studied it well.

◆◆◆

artila devi. (24, suva, fiji)

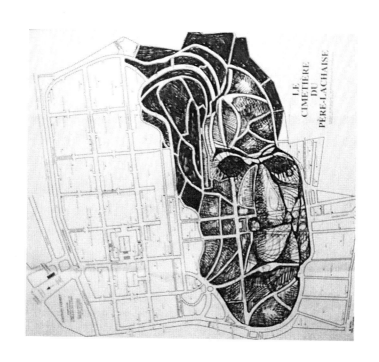

face in the cemetery. by joão machado. (27, rio de janeiro, brazil)

the incessant writings of an uneducated woman

by alanna davis-robins

I was a woman who wanted peace with my man. Being a Black woman and witnessing the waging war between Black men and Black women in the sphere of love, sex, money, and respect, I wanted to love and support him. Give him what he could not get anywhere else, not even from within himself. I still feel this way; the problem was that I compromised myself along the way. I find myself carrying many burdens, but none bigger than what has since become the defining moment in my evolution. At the age of twenty-four, never did I think I would have conceived twice in three months, and not be a mother. With broken spirit, every day was pained with guilt and remorse of irreparable errors. Somehow, unwittingly, I got caught up in a war of the sexes, of ideals, of unrequited love - and I still don't know how.

The grief of what transpired manifested itself through physical malfunctions and emotional breakdowns, intensified acid-reflux disease, amplified gallbladder disease, an inability to sleep through most nights, a year-long abnormal menstruation cycle, increased teeth grinding, gripping depression, haunting inquisitive dreams, and anxiety attacks. I contemplated death and thought that some sort of torture was appropriate as I remained part of a physical embodiment of what my children would have been.

I felt unbearably sick for three weeks in July 2003, just before I began graduate school. One Friday, I went to the doctor and learned I was pregnant. It was surprising how easy it was for me to decide to have an abortion and go through with it the following Friday.

The surgery was more physically than emotionally painful. I was alone for the operation and afterward, surprisingly, there were no feelings of remorse. The next day, there were pro-life protestors in front of City Hall, carrying pictures of aborted fetuses. It was shocking and emotionally draining - but, still, there was no regret. At twenty-two I could barely take care of myself, let alone a baby.

In January of 2005, as I started my last semester of graduate school, I discovered that I was pregnant for the second time. This time there was a bit of uncertainty. I didn't know where to turn, what to do, or where to go. Even now it's a blur. My boyfriend, Adam, and I reluctantly decided that abortion would again be the best alternative. I was often depressed, crying uncontrollably, and feeling as if I was literally suffocating.

I am a naturally private person and I couldn't face telling my friends about my predicament, so Adam made plans to travel from Chicago to Pittsburgh to support me during the procedure. Unfortunately, the soonest he could get off work was mid-February and, when morning sickness finally got the best of me, I once again found myself alone at the doctor's office. There would be no one there to drive me home, pick up my antibiotics and pain medication, cook me food, hold my hand, give me a hug, talk to me, sit in silence with me… nothing.

The second surgery was much more physically excruciating. The doctor had to stop and continue again because I kept moving. I stopped for medicine and food on my way home, and I was determined to relax for the remainder of the day. Adam didn't call. By the time the phone finally rang that night, my anger had welled up to the point where I was ready to chop off his head. Adam said he didn't think I was actually going to go through with the procedure, and thought I was going to wait until he arrived. After quarreling, he stated he was not coming down at all.

About a month after the second procedure I had a dream in which I was a mother of two twins. Most of the surroundings were white, and I was lying on a bed holding two babies. They looked just like my twin sister and me at the time of our birth, extremely tiny with pale pink skin.

Looking through my friend's dream book and reading its interpretation of the dream was amazing, enlightening, and shameful. The book stated that, in Eastern cultures, white represents death. I soon realized the babies were the two I had conceived, but never birthed. I only told Adam about the dream. It was a lingering reminder of what had happened and a clear rationalization of wrongs I couldn't correct. As the weeks passed I continued to feel discomfort permeating all areas of my life. I feared the disgrace and dishonor would never wane.

The third conception, and the end of my love, would haunt me most. A month and a half had passed since my second procedure, and I was in dire need of companionship. After waiting weeks for Adam to come, I decided to travel from Pittsburgh to Chicago by train to see him. Upon arrival, I was surprised at his cool demeanor. Emotionally, he treated me as if I was a stranger. Physically, however, he looked at me like a piece of meat. After refusing to give into his sexual desires for most of the night, Adam appeared to respect my decision. After a few drinks, however, he couldn't hear a word I said.

All I wanted was comfort - for him to listen, to validate my pain in some way. After saying no three times, somehow my legs unwillingly, robotically spread and he entered. For weeks, I was intoxicated with grief and unreasonably hoped he could help lessen the pain. Though it was not a physical rape, I do feel it was an emotional rape. Upon returning to school, I immediately went to the medical center to get the day-after pill, continually in a state of unrelenting solitude.

Everything was fine until I went to the doctor for a pap smear a few weeks later, and the nurse decided to take a urine sample. She then walked in and told me that I was pregnant (again) in a berating, scolding tone. I looked at her in disbelief. As I left the building, I called Adam crying. It had been two weeks since I last spoke to him. I remember telling him how I hated him for what happened. I had now been pregnant for the second time in three months.

Feeling betrayed by my ex and by myself, I was paralyzed, constantly weeping, and filled with rage, fear, and panic. Nonetheless, I told Adam that I was determined to keep this child. I had already given up two and was not going to give up another, no discussion. Graduation and finals were fast approaching, but

the incessant writings of an uneducated woman

I could not concentrate on school.

All I could think about was how I got to this place. I looked in the mirror wondering who the person was staring back at me. Five years ago I would have refused to have an abortion, but here I was - pregnant for the third time in nineteen months. I kept telling myself this was not me; that this was not my life.

After finals, I moved back into my parents' house in Chicago and I broke the news to them. Still unaware of my first two pregnancies, they would later say I moved in with the deliberate intention to mislead them and they therefore felt justified in pressuring me to end the pregnancy.

My mother was somewhat supportive until my dad found out. I assume that, to some, my father's reaction was rational; he told that me I would not have a baby in his house. He then began bullying me into having an abortion. He wasn't the only one; Adam joined his crusade. Thankfully, my cousin and close friend were constantly there to hear every new update about my father yelling at me or calling me, in a word, a loser. I also had the support of my sister, who took me in when my father kicked me out.

Come mid-July, however, I was twenty weeks into the pregnancy and my father and Adam were adamant about me going to a clinic despite my wishes. Although I am certain that my father hated Adam for getting his little girl pregnant, it felt as if they were working together against me. To appease them, with no intention of going through with the procedure, I scheduled a time at the only place in Chicago where I could get an appointment for an abortion halfway into the pregnancy.

It was a Thursday. Adam went to work for the first half of the day and met me at the clinic where I was greeted by three protestors who were eager to tell me about the "murder" the center commits. We went inside and were summoned to the back with a counselor who explained this would be a three-day procedure, and wanted to ensure that I understood everything it entailed. Unlike the first two, I would need to be placed under general anesthesia this time. I signed forms stating that I was doing this of my own volition, thereby excusing the clinic of any liability if something went wrong. In my mind, the only reason I was signing the papers was to appease Adam, who was right there with me to ensure the procedure occurred.

quarter passed

Following the explanation and warnings, it was time to pay - $900. That was twice the cost of my two previous procedures combined. At this point, I told Adam I was ready to go, but he refused to leave.

Abortion is part of the politics of being female. The fact that I was a Black woman in this situation involved the misguided politics and mistaken assumptions of me being a sexually overt jezebel, that I could not somehow constrain myself to the measures of birth control. It involves the polemics of welfare, a single-parent home, and producing children that can help the cause rather than contribute to the problem.

I had no job, health insurance, or support for that matter, and I was pregnant by a man I no longer loved. Then, of course, there was also the stigma surrounding my traditional middle class family, the loss of pride and expression of disappointment from my parents, and the financial encumbrance on those around me. And I knew that I would not be able to give the baby all that I hoped to give. I could feel myself starting to doubt, starting to falter. Could I really take care of my child?

Adam did not even have enough money to pay for half. I tendered payment for an abortion I did not want. Again, like so many times before, I did all I could to hold back the tears.

I thought, "Maybe if I let them fall, this woman would see how I really feel."

Maybe if I had told her that I did not want to terminate my baby - that I was just there under the pressure of my parents and Adam - she would have counseled me, and led me to the door. After the first day, I had the option of changing my mind, but I was afraid of the consequences and potential complications so I continued with the termination. Like a robot, I silently bowed my head and submitted again.

Saturday, there were protestors again. I was finally called, and the doctor and I only exchanged a few words. I was asleep almost immediately. It was difficult to wake up in the recovery room but when I awoke, I felt the difference in my body immediately. My baby was gone and all of a sudden it was so real. There was an instantaneous feeling of dread. I laid a hand on my abdomen, but there was nothing. During sporadic bouts of consciousness, I kept asking myself if this was actually happening.

I demanded to see the doctor. In my panicked state, I needed to know how the procedure went. I needed to hear from him that after three abortions, I would still be able to have children. In a passive voice he assured me that everything was fine and that he did not foresee any complications with future pregnancies. Leaving, shielding my eyes from the blinding sun, Adam and I drove by the crowd of screaming protestors.

The next night I dreamt I was at a friend's bachelorette party and a girl said to the bride-to-be, "I know why you're rushing the wedding. It's obvious you're pregnant." I started crying uncontrollably in my sleep; so hard that I actually woke myself.

I felt like a monster. I believed I had cemented my place in hell, if there was one. My life felt like leftovers of the life I once had. The only thing getting me through was the possibility of having children in the future. I even lied to friends, telling them that I had miscarried the baby. I couldn't explain it and I couldn't erase it. I have nothing but scars and memories of what could have been. As time passed, with the bereavement of it all, I slowly started to feel that sanity was escaping me.

I spent the next six months after the abortion in a fragile, trance-like state. Every day, I was broken again. I soon left Chicago and moved to Washington, D.C. There, I did seek therapy and initially I had to wait three months to get an appointment for intake. When I heard that I started crying. They agreed to see me for as long as they could at an emergency clinic.

After explaining what happened, I felt that my therapist, much like the few people in my life who knew my story, did not understand. She would give me quizzical looks as if to say, "Many women have abortions, so what's the problem?" Though my doctor never voiced such a query, my cousin and his girlfriend constantly did. It seemed that no one would ever understand, but I soon realized no one cared to understand. I was not a victim; I was a young woman whose poor decisions led her to a ghastly place, and no one wanted to identify with someone like that. We all make choices every day and my choices led me to a state of utter despondency and

quarter passed

anguish.

The therapist felt I should be on some type of medication so she gave me anti-depressants to use during the day and a sedative to help me sleep. Six weeks later, I stopped taking the anti-depressants. I did not like the idea of numbing the pain just to be competent during the day. Anxiety attacks began, but I needed to feel it all.

As I started recovery, I planned to leave no holes, no soft spots, and no spores for self-hatred or self-doubt to seep into the unguarded regions of my internal being. I told a cousin how I had fallen from grace and failed in what had been, up to that point, the ultimate test of my character. She suggested that the true test of my character would be how I responded to the situation now. That stuck.

I need no justification, no sympathy. I just want those who understand, or who identify through their own personal circumstances, to know that there is a way forward. Often times, I still feel as if sanity is escaping me, but when I think of peace from this war that has been raging within, I think of fitting into my skin.

On my birthday this past August, I dreamt I was nine months pregnant. I was not visibly happy, but I felt content and very much at ease. In the dream, I started going into labor, but I was not in pain. That was the first day of my present life.

alanna davis-robins. (27, fairfax station, virginia, usa)

seclusion. by archie p. valdez. (26, long beach, new york, usa)

# no airplanes in the sky

by kelley calvert

Lightning bugs burst into tiny lights in the Indiana sky. The air heavy with humidity held the lights in place, luminous in the dark. The insects communicated in glowing electrical code, programmed by thousands of years of evolution to seek a mate.

We saw only the light of their intentions at Arbuckle Acre Park on my seventh birthday. Our parents had given us lightning bug catchers, devices that consisted of a clear plastic tube and a pink lid sprinkled with air holes. Now, instead of just catching fireflies and letting them go, we had a measure of progress.

"Look! I've caught twenty-four fireflies!"

"So? I have at least a hundred!"

The bugs were about a half-inch long with black, angular wings and red, beady heads. They were often mangled during the pursuit, exhibiting broken wings and goo, the aftermath of children's enthusiasm. Of course, we grew tired of chasing these tiny lights and the cages lay forgotten overnight. The following morning, it was a strange lesson to uncover a bottle of dead bugs. It brought the mystery and instinctive fear of death to the forefront.

It also illustrated the tendency of living things to die in captivity.

Everyone knows exactly where they were the day of September 11th. Except you; you don't. You missed it by three weeks. I remember exactly where I was the moment you died: Wheeling, West Virginia. I was driving to Indy from D.C. because you were in the hospital. You were technically alive for two more days, but I felt you leave the earth then. It was as tangible, as real as losing a physical part

no airplanes in the sky

of my being.

It was a square, yellow room. Anonymous. I was working a temporary, mindless job. I worked in a cubicle surrounded by a hundred other squares. I was the fastest producer with "the least errors, in the top 5% of employees." I was very happy making someone else money with my efficiency. The lunchroom was color-coded. Black people sat on one side and white people sat on the other. I was narcoleptic at the time, so I spent twenty minutes a day sound asleep in my car.

After I woke up, I bought coffee and read the paper for five minutes.
One day, there was a story about an elephant orphanage in Nairobi. If their mothers are poached, elephant calves will actually lie down and die of starvation next to their mothers rather than live without them. And when played the sounds made by former acquaintances, elephants become hysterical. They search their surroundings for the source of this acoustical apparition. Their sadness and confusion over hearing one assumed lost or dead becomes apparent in their frantic searching. After I read this story, I put my head down on the table and started sobbing. The cruelty of being human was somehow captured in that moment.
The curse of humans is the memory of an elephant.

In the days following September 11th, an eerie silence filled everything. There were no airplanes in the sky. The stillness of the air snuck into the pauses in conversation. It crept up behind you in a car with its brights on in the middle of the night. It followed you into dreams. It was remaining visual evidence that there had been an attack - that evil was a real thing.
I was living in the outskirts, huddled in the hinterlands of Washington D.C. I found myself driving along the highway thinking that if only an airplane would pass overhead, everything would return to normal. Just one airplane. When they passed however in the days to follow, roaring mightily overhead, they were nothing but military jets guarding the holy city.
Our president's voice echoed down the valley of revenge. We would make the world go blind because we were so furious over the silence.

quarter passed

I wanted to escape.

In the streets of Accra, white skin marks you as a foreigner. You start to wish that you were darker so that you could blend into the humming background. Taxis rush past humans swarming through traffic fraught with fumes, dodging a man selling jump-ropes who is delighted because you speak French and he is from Burkina Faso, through child prostitutes and old expatriate men, past a woman crippled by polio begging for money.

At one of the endless booths of people hawking necklaces, drums, sculptures, masks, paintings, I found a chess set that seemed to be made out of ivory. I asked the young artisan behind the counter, "Is this ivory?"

"Yeah," he said.

"Why would you even sell this?" I asked, "Don't you realize what the price of this is?"

I was immediately ashamed by the question. The vendor started laughing.

I had just read a historical account of colonization of the Congo in which there were photographs of grand Belgian men with big mustaches and starchy uniforms standing proudly next to large piles of tusks. The Africans had learned from the best. Rich white people all over the world are willing to pay gobs of money for something that has the gruesome appeal of Nazi memorabilia.

The world runs on supply and demand.

When the trumpets of war sounded, we all darted into alleyways to hide like stray cats, lowered our voices at work when we discussed politics, looked over our shoulders on the subway. It was a time of paranoia. Your neighbor is a terrorist. Orange alert. Get out the duct tape and saran wrap, dear. Scientists have documented the first case of computer to human transmission of bird flu. Don't forget your daily multi-vitamin. Red alert.

The roar preceded the apparition. I was sitting on the mountain that hugged the eastern corner of my small village in Benin. In the plain below, patches of deforestation complained of their emptiness while brown grew around them. White birds moved from one end of the world to the other. Lizards scrambled clumsily past in the underbrush. I would sit for hours there, just watching and listening.

When I heard the sound, I looked around me, searching for the source. I wondered briefly if West Africa experiences earthquakes. When a tiny glimmer of silver reflected off the distant skyline, I realized that I had been completely bewildered by a sound once so familiar.

I followed the airplane with my eyes hungrily. It was a remnant of a place that I had not seen in two years. It was a morsel of a world that I had lost, left behind over endless water and time. I imagined coffee, metropolitan bliss, comfort. No more illness. No more death.

That airplane was going to a world to which I could never return, a world unaware of drought, a world that knows where its next meal is coming from, a world of one-car-per-person, a world of driving-thru and not making eye contact, a world where the silence has been filled with just-buy-its and googling the senses out of information, a world full of everything and somehow full of nothing.

Tony Blair and Bono see an end to poverty. I do not.

The day after my twenty-seventh birthday, my neighbor, Amina, lost her mother in a taxi crash. I was so astonished by the amount of death around me that my journal entries devolved into lists.

- 24 June
Eight Dead in the Crash:
    Amina's mother
    Fati from the health center
    Sofo's carpenter friend, his wife and child
    Chauffer
    Two people I don't know
Visited Amina's family. Covered the mundane details of death. Somehow describing particulars, we forget death's finality. I couldn't look at Amina too long. Her suffering was everywhere.

quarter passed

There was a time when I vowed to myself to record your story, but when I tried, I collapsed into Ground Zero. I was walking against a biting wind that only America's northeast can muster, freezing crosswinds that chatter in laughter at your jacket. Tears were freezing to my face. I had hit bottom. I thought to myself that one day I would tell your story, our story, but I couldn't speak in that silence. Everything was buried in dreams. I dreamt of terrorist bombs falling on D.C., the mistaken city in which I lived. I dreamt of being buried alive with you. I dreamt of meeting you for a drink in Indianapolis.

For months I saw you in the crowd. I saw you at the mall in the line of faces rising from the escalator. Later, I saw you in the tangle of African faces rushing past at the market where voodooists say the dead walk amongst the living.

The distance between cultures is largest in vacuums, where words fail. Add that silence to the silence of living and dying in different worlds. As it turns out, capturing the mundane details of death is much easier than capturing the mundane details of life. Death holds still and lets you look at it longer.

I had ten minutes alone with you before they cut life support. I told you all the details of my life, that I had left D.C., that I was moving to California, that I would be going to Africa as a Peace Corps Volunteer. I started talking and couldn't stop. I wanted to capture all the stories that had passed, all the stories that were coming. I wanted to capture the rest of my life in those tiny moments. I watched the monitors that carried the rhythm of your breathing, the beating of your heart, the activity of your brain. I looked for a response to my voice. I didn't see any.

Voices are one of those things that carry. We remember voices and carry them with us as keys to our memories. They say we acquire every sound we will ever be able to produce by the age of four. Imagine a world where voice acquisition was the same.

You'd recognize the voices of your mother, father, some siblings and scattered relatives… but everything after that would be a shadow, your memory always searching the voice of a stranger for something familiar to hang on to. Every lover's voice would be eternally new. No song would ever be redundant, no favorite band lost to over-familiarity. Every sound would flourish in the springtime of its life: green and bursting with promise.

    This might just be the voice to carry you home.

kelley calvert. (28, salinas, california, usa)

quarter passed

sunset. by adrianus smith, jr. (26, windhoek, namibia)

6

career

rejection. by sarah nelson. (25, paris, france)

the rejection collection
by sarah nelson

Visitors to my apartment always spend an unusually long time in the bathroom. This does not concern me, as I know what they are doing - reading. No, they are not fascinated by the stack of New Yorker's on the back of the toilet or the ingredients of my hand soap. My bathroom walls are papered with uncommon reading material: rejection letters from magazines, editors, and literary agents, collected while attempting to publish my fiction.

Guests always emerge from the bathroom impressed. Many have chosen a favorite. Some puzzle over the koan-like contradictions in one letter. "How can something be both vague and over-detailed?" One woman confessed, "I've never gotten a rejection letter." I immediately offered her one.

The letters are arranged casually, taped up in the order in which I received them. One corner showcases a collage of various rejections from an editor known for his swiftness, promptness and lacerative skill. Another wall is devoted to full-page rejections, missives filled with florid apologies. The smaller notes, from literary magazines so poorly funded that they can only afford to send eighth-sized rejection slips, are arranged around the mirror on the door. This contrast serves as a humbling reminder; my reflected image is surrounded by phrases such as "The return of your work does not necessarily imply criticism of its merit." No, but do I look fat in these pants?

My first rejection came from a magazine editor for whom a high school classmate interned during our senior year. I slipped my friend a manuscript, an absurd tale of a nun who becomes pregnant and hitchhikes to North Carolina, with instructions to pass it on. The editor, in a note addressed to my friend, pointed out the "problems of credibility," but amended, "This woman has talent." I was overjoyed - he called me a woman! At seventeen, this was more than a late-blooming young writer could ask for.

Before I mounted the collection, rejections used to get me down. I would scrutinize the checkmark in the "Please try us again" box on form letters. Was it checked with enthusiasm? Did the editor really mean it? I even considered retaliation. My rejection of the rejection would go something like:

"Dear Editor, While your letter is very moving, I cannot give your rejection the necessary enthusiasm it deserves. I am confident you will find another writer who will be more receptive to your rejection. All best, etc."

Now, with each returned self-addressed stamped envelope, I simply tear off another piece of tape and continue assembling my masterpiece of interior design.

Others have offered to contribute to the tour de force, but I tell them to start their own collections. One friend has a marvelous stack of rejections of his first novel, several addressed to names that bear no resemblance to his, one headed with the caveat, "I thought you might like to see what a recent college graduate had to say about your manuscript," one signed by a person named "Xanthe."

Am I the first to create such a shrine to my artistic failure? Rumor had it T.S. Eliot engaged in a similar activity, but a friend assures me that Eliot never received a single rejection letter, never mind a wall's worth. I've seen those clever books of famous rejections, of course, and read with proper smugness the struggles of various canonical writers to publish their first books. But rejection as art, as affirmation? This, surely, is something new.

The walls are nearly filled, at least the spaces far enough from the shower not to be destroyed by it. The paper has started to yellow and curl from the humidity; some rejections last longer than others.

I've been apartment hunting lately, looking to relocate when my lease runs out at the end of the month. I'd like a less slanted floor, higher ceilings, maybe a gas stove, but one feature most of all - a bigger bathroom.

◆◆◆

sarah nelson. (25, paris, france)

nameless and faceless

by peter ryan

I envy you, sitting in the bathroom stall. Your world is six feet by four feet right now, with nothing visible all around you except your personal confines. I don't know where you work, who your supervisor is, or what your co-workers think of you. You could be an intern or my boss. You could be the janitor or the CEO. You are a nameless, faceless pair of shoes. You're momentarily anonymous.

You have no known history; you have no foreseeable future. I don't know how long you have worked in this building or if you'll be fired tomorrow. I don't see the problems that have been following you around all day. I can't anticipate who or what will be waiting for you once you get home. You were there when I came in and you're still there after I leave. You're momentarily eternal.

You simply exist, unknown to anyone currently outside of these walls, the king of the small world you inhabit. No one will bother you here, no one will ridicule your work, no one will tell you what to do. No one will ask you when the report will be ready. No one will guilt you into coming to company outings. No one will pawn their work off on you. You're momentarily invincible.

You can't see me from in there either. You don't know me. You don't judge me, you don't pressure me, you don't bother me, you don't expect from me. You won't comment on my bad haircut, you won't look over my shoulder while I'm working. You won't ask me how I'm doing, and then proceed to tell me all your problems instead. You're momentarily my best friend.

You have a life outside that stall, but it doesn't exist to me. You're completely anonymous. You'll eventually leave and go back to your world and your problems. You'll have someone monitoring your progress, asking you to do something when you're free, but by COB today. You may be a saint; you may be an asshole. You

nameless and faceless

may be an ideal father; you may beat your wife. You may volunteer every Saturday; you might enjoy hitting small animals with your gas guzzling SUV. You may come out of that stall, see the pain in my eyes, and wonder what the hell is wrong with me. For now, however, you're momentarily perfect.

◆◆◆

peter ryan. (25, danbury, connecticut, usa)

quarter passed

pilgrims. by dixon bordiano. (20, minneapolis, minnesota, usa)

boiling milk
by wade forrest wilson

With the final squirts of cooking oil on the grill, I stood still for the first time in three hours. I waited for the heated hiss to die down before I ran a porous scraper across the vertical lines of the grill. Cleaning off charred remains of seared steaks, chicken breasts and burgers, I wiped my forehead with the only unsoiled space on my kitchen uniform, which was specifically intended for the cleaning of my brow perspiration.

The grill can be the most intense job in an eating establishment. Many people would argue that the bartender has the most demanding job, but these people haven't stood over a scorching 350° C grill during the hottest days of summer while catering to the burger-loving populace that chooses T.G.I. Friday's as their early dinner choice.

In kitchen jargon it's called "getting slammed," the time when all hell breaks loose behind the scenes, a chaotic assembly of cooks, frantically lost in the fray, slipping on trampled romaine lettuce and smearing stranded fries across the greasy tiled floor as they attempt to stem the flow of orders that keep coming in. But new bills keep printing, creating a curtain of white slips waving in the warm air being stirred up by the useless fan next to my grill.

This job is killing me. I started out in the dish pit and after two weeks of menial, dirty, steamy slavery, I was promoted to the fryer. What a fun job that was, getting burned from snapping boiling oil every five minutes as the frozen water crystals on the jalapeño poppers spit wicked, spiced fluid onto my skin. From there, I worked the soups, salads and sandwiches - a posh little food station that didn't require much skill or pain tolerance. During each of these promotions, I felt like I was going somewhere.

The T.G.I. Friday's management team would make annual sojourns to Dallas, Texas, to learn how to effectively brainwash each employee into thinking his or

quarter passed

her job is meaningful, that he or she has potential. These little promotions were a part of the company plan; each time you advanced from a horrible station to a slightly less horrible station, you felt empowered that you had taken another step towards your successful future.

And so here I was, working the last step on the kitchen ladder - the grill. On the grill, you have to demonstrate your ability to cope with lunch and dinner slams to make it past this last rung. Slaving away here means that you can handle kitchen stress and create safely cooked, quality food.

Imagine fifteen burgers of different varieties and twelve sirloin steaks (four of which are teriyaki, six are Jack Daniels-sauced, and two that are steak spiced) that need to be grilled to one of seven degrees of cooked preference. Add that to eight chicken breasts, seven orders of skewered prawns, five salmon steaks, three veggie burgers, five orders of fajitas, six slabs of BBQ baby back ribs and fifteen minutes to cook it and, all of a sudden, you have a disaster that's only one over-cooked steak away from catastrophe.

The pressure, combined with the heat and the dexterity required to rotate all this food in such a manner, has caused many a cook to demote himself to an easier and less stressful position. I was too proud to take a step back. I could handle the stress, but I couldn't handle not being given the monetary respect I felt I deserved. I could not be comfortable getting paid $8.25 when I knew that the restaurant's success depended heavily on my abilities to cook the patrons' food. Without me, there was no restaurant, or, at least, I tried to convince myself of this while I swayed in exhausted delirium, marveling at my clean and empty grill. It is a beautiful sight when you've worked so hard for so long without ever seeing it empty. But such is the case in…

"Boys, boys!" the conceited hostess piped. She hesitated when she initially didn't see anyone on the food line. They all had left for their cigarette break. I didn't smoke; that pleased management because they didn't think I had any legitimate excuse to be outside taking a break.

"Hey, Kitchen!" She half-yelled as she finally caught glimpse of me in the corner by the grill.

I nodded my chin to signal, "What." I was too tired and pissed off to make any effort to talk.

"Just thought I'd, like, you know, letcha know that, like, there's like one table of like twenty-five people, and, um, another party just like showed up now and have like thirty people."

She popped one sharp Hubba Bubba-bubble, pivoted and left without waiting for a response, which wasn't coming anyway. But still, what nerve!

Our five minute reprieve ended with the cursed sound of the printer squelching out an order. After ten seconds the printer hadn't stopped, I instinctively froze. Fifteen seconds and the printer persisted. It kept buzzing. Twenty seconds! A sickening sensation entered the pit of my stomach, the kind procrastinators get when they sit in front of a fifteen page research essay knowing they can't leave that chair until it is finished.

At thirty seconds the printer momentarily halted and snipped off the food bill. I picked it up; it was the length of my leg. To my utter astonishment, it all required the grill - except for one Caesar Salad. I presumed it was some American tour group (those damn carnivorous Yanks!) and that the salad must be for their Canadian guide. I realized, to my dismay, that there was no point in calling in the rest of the crew when I had to do all the orders.

In vacant silence my mind pulsated with the desire to blow. To lose it. Perform the ever-so-popular kitchen walkout. Talk to any cook and he will tell you about the guy he witnessed do it. The episode usually involves the smashing of a few plates or the kicking of a few pots - minimal damage in the larger sense, but imagine the excitement of the remaining staff. They have all fantasized about sticking it to the management after being taken advantage of and neglected for so long. Just witnessing someone else do it would be liberating enough to keep them going for at least another couple of weeks.

I knew I had to make a decision quickly. I equate the feeling to the boiling of milk. There comes a certain point where the milk will no longer gently bubble, but will either explode in a growing cloud of froth that expands and spills over the pot's edge, or it must be removed from the heat entirely where it can calm and cool. I couldn't stay in the slow simmering boil I was in; the heat was beginning to become overwhelming. Should I boil over and make my frustration known

quarter passed

with pieces of broken crockery?

But then, through my fatigue, it dawned on me. I had the opportunity to be better than the cheap management. I would prove to myself that I could bear the weight of the entire restaurant and still produce a product that would satisfy each and every customer. And I did. For the entire night tirelessly, calmly, poised, I was driven to complete my work with Zen-like focus. But, as the shift drew to a close, I wondered how long such a relationship could last between me and this grill. It is very tiring being a cook because all you do is give-out. Very rarely do you get anything in return and if you do, it is usually because you failed to cook a steak to satisfaction.

That night I gave my two week's notice, happy with the knowledge that in my absence this establishment would finally recognize that I was worth more than $8.25. I knew that my calmness and perseverance would provide me with the only thing I could hope to gain from them and from this situation - my integrity.

I just let the milk simmer.

◆◆◆

wade forrest wilson. (30, langley, british columbia, canada)

last chance road. by mike o'donnell. (25, seattle, washington, usa)

quarter passed

ode to the office
by jessica watson

You broken bride of necessity
You grey-walled malapert tramp
Your somnolent whirrings, you subtle bitch
Copier, fax machine, stamps.
Your paper white skirts and ink toner touch
The cuckolded kept-man mock
Your nine-to-five dance, that eight hour tease
Computer screen, coffee pot, clock.

jessica watson. (24, toronto, ontario, canada)

desempleo
by carol j. thomas

Two days ago, I received a pink slip. I was surprised and shocked, having put all my hopes and dreams into working for a top multinational corporation where I saw myself growing as a professional and gaining valuable experience. I don't need to tell you that I quickly found myself overrun by a great sadness regarding my future, which appeared to me a dark, uncertain wasteland. I wondered how I would overcome my doubts, start interviewing for jobs again, and tell my friends and family that I was unemployed. I thought about it all weekend, struggling to stave off depression. For the second time in my life, I felt utterly alone.

My mother obtained her Green Card in 2000 and she and my sixteen year-old brother were off to the United States, leaving Panama - and me - behind. I could not join them because, at twenty-two years of age, I was too old to be considered a dependent. When my family reached the U.S., my mother submitted the paperwork to facilitate my emigration; seven years later, we are still waiting for a response.

In casual conversation, I prefer not to divulge many details about my private life or my living situation. On those few, rare occasions when I do admit to living alone, I try to cut short the barrage of prying questions that usually follows.

Is the house my property? No comment.
Do I pay the mortgage? I pay to live here.
How long have I lived alone? Long enough.
Why do I live alone? Just because…

At first, it was strange to enter my mother's house and find it to be so empty. I never thought that I would miss my family so much. But I do, and during Christmas, New Year's Eve and other special occasions, I feel their absence the most. Living without them makes me reflect upon my own humanity and my own nature.

quarter passed

Although I am very much an independent woman, I feel a strong connection to my family, even with the distance. Still, over time, I have adapted to my condition and I have gotten used to being on my own. I have spent the past eight years occupied with my studies, earning my business administration degree, and my career. It was in these things that I felt comfort and security.

I live a few hundred kilometers from the office and, over the past several months, I commuted five to six hours each day to earn my way as an executive assistant. I was out of the house by 5:10 a.m. each morning, and I often did not return home until 11:00 p.m. each night, only to go to bed and begin the cycle anew hours later. I had consistently demonstrated my dedication to the job and to the company, and I had hoped to make it my career, but it was not meant to be.

After the initial shock wore off, I decided that my misfortune was a chance to change my life. I always try to stay positive, to think that tomorrow will be better. I'm certain that the road, although it may appear rocky and impassible today, can be transformed and re-paved tomorrow. Unemployment has given me the opportunity to figure out my next step and ponder a future that I have considered for some time.

I have decided to accept a job in another environment, one that lays in stark contrast to the frantic lifestyle of the city. I'll live on an island I know, far from the city. I have always wanted to move away, but professional aspirations and personal obligations always kept me from doing so. Yes, I was content with my mundane job and lonely existence. But, wasn't I happier knowing that the possibility of escape existed? Although conventional wisdom dictates that I should search for another city job, my heart yearns for a change of scenery, a new set of challenges, and a more relaxed lifestyle.

I have spent the past eight years waiting for change, and although this is not the change I expected, I see that there is no better time for me to make a change and follow my desires than now. I'm not afraid of taking this step forward, nor do I fear failure. Circumstance has finally given me an opening to follow a new path.

I picked up the phone this morning and made a call. With my mother's blessing, nothing is impossible.

◆◆◆

carol j. thomas.   (29, panama city, panama)

untitled. by maryam gerling salassi. (23, euless, texas, usa)

quarter passed

forgetting yourself
by katherine chamberlain

How do you make the decision, the transition,
From cool to professional,
From department store clearance racks to a woman with stockings and skirt suits?
Ringing telephones and inboxes over size limit;
Fearing marriage proposals or the lack thereof;
Accepting that the person sitting across from you thinks you're dumb.
Days of calling in sick to make appointments for spa treatments
I can't even afford.

katherine chamberlain. (26, washington, district of columbia, usa)

the mouth above my door

by hava helan

    Before I open the door to my apartment, I see the mouth, wide open. Even in the dark, it signals me home. Every time I round the corner, I watch how it approaches me, gets bigger and bigger, and then it's above my head. I take out the key from my pocket, put it in the lock and enter. A dentist works downstairs in the basement of my building. Somehow, this dentist's sign has become my own.

    It is pink; a few teeth are missing. The upper and lower front teeth have been replaced by letters. These letters skim the tongue, announcing the existence of the dentist's office. Otherwise the sign looks like someone is yelling, or maybe yawning. The mouth is suspended in midair like the Cheshire Cat's grin. The ears haven't appeared, yet, nor has the rest; there's no one to talk to. It may turn out that I'm actually living in someone.

    I've never seen the dentist. I've been thinking about him, though. About the profession. How dentists work intimately inside the oral cavity. How they often cause temporary discomfort, but it's a necessary pain. How they bend over, look inside, get inside, where hardly anyone else ever does. The dentist and I have a lot in common. He maintains and repairs teeth over time, while I develop the tongue. When we open up mouths, people often speak funny; they're not used to the intrusion. He inserts instruments, foreign objects; I insert a foreign language. He fills cavities, I tell my clients to fill-in-the-blanks.

    In both dentistry and grammar, there is a corrective element. Orthodontics and orthography enhance your outward appearance. Your smile and speech must project an image of confidence. Aesthetics and phonetics must meet global standards. Each visit to us is an investment; the improvement in your mouth carries a promise.

quarter passed

If you are Eastern European, from the former communist bloc, and are able to speak English, you can pronounce your independence. You have a new lease on life. I've helped a few young Polish students wanting to learn this universal language; some hoping to conquer the West, others just wishing to lead a decent life with some job security. I need them as they need me. Then the day comes when they become proficient enough.

Whether or not they leave Poland, they all eventually leave me. I'm not complaining. I'm unemployed, but my pocket diary still has some meetings and deadlines in it. (I view one page at a time not to panic.) This creates a sense of irregularity I don't altogether dislike. Besides, I can pay my bills.

I listen. I talk. Translate. Explain, revise, correct, clarify, teach. It's what I do for my living. I delve and fumble for words, the right words. It never stops. I converse. In my sleep. I write. I literally (and literarily) live from hand to mouth. Yes, the open mouth is also my sign.

I'm like the dentist. We benefit from what ails people - what aches, the growing or decayed instruments of speech. Our clients want a check-up, need to see improvement, and they can pay. Their treatments depend on their economic status, no doubt. Have they eaten too many sweets as children? Do they have to emigrate? Or maybe it's vanity. The improvement is suspended high, like the sign of the gaping mouth. Or the Cheshire Cat's grin. The pink tongue truly should stick out at me. I expect it to happen every time I come home.

Whenever I see the mouth, silent, speechless, stuffed with letters, I think, it would be worthwhile to fill this emptiness with words.

hava helan. (26, kraków, poland)

tainted
by andrew blackman

The things I touch seem tainted. That's the best way that I can describe how I feel as my twenties draw to a close. Sure, I've moved beyond adolescent nihilism, but I haven't yet found satisfaction from my young adulthood either. It's something in-between. It's a sense that although there are things in life that I believe in very strongly and that I would like to achieve, the achievement of them would give me less satisfaction because of what I now know.

For example, I started out wanting to make money – lots of it. And I succeeded. By the age of twenty-one I got a job in London with the world's largest bank, and by twenty-two I was transferred to New York, making a six-figure salary. By twenty-three I had my own office on the eighteenth floor of a Wall Street office building, and by twenty-five, I quit.

After that, because I wanted to do something more meaningful, I went into journalism. Thanks to my banking background I was able to get a job as a reporter at *The Wall Street Journal*. For a while, life was much better, and I even thought I would be able to make reporting my long-term career. But two years later I quit and moved back to London with the idea of concentrating on getting my first novel published and writing a second.

In other words, at the age of twenty-nine, I am back where I was when my twenties began: living with my parents with no income and an abundance of dreams with no direction. Of course, I know how this must sound. Poor little rich kid, whining because he had so many opportunities and didn't know which one to take. And, in a sense, that was always the problem.

When I was at Citigroup, I found myself consumed by a curious, but extremely powerful, sense of shame. I just couldn't fathom how it was possible to pick up thousands of dollars a week without much strain when I knew that the majority of the world was making one or two dollars a day for labouring ten times as hard. In fact, I didn't even have to look to distant lands: New York City is a microcosm of everything that is wrong with the world - and my place in it. Even within my own office building, I have perfect examples of the oppressive disparity between myself and the Others: the security guards, the cleaners, the mailroom guys, the cafeteria workers. Then, on my way home, I have constant reminders of the have-nots: the people who drive my taxis, shine my shoes, serve my pizza, open the door of my plush apartment building. I could look at them and know that every one of them would work their entire life and probably never earn as much as I did as a twenty-two year old.

And what did I do to deserve this lofty position in life? Not enough. It's true that I didn't have it all served to me on a silver platter as some people do. I had to work hard to get a good education from a prestigious school. After that, however, the word "Oxford" on my CV has opened doors that would otherwise have remained firmly closed. No matter the fact that I received a degree in History. For example, when I interviewed with Citigroup's Global Corporate and Investment Bank at the age of twenty-one, I didn't know a bond from a share - and had absolutely no interest in knowing. Yet, I still got a job usually reserved for people with MBAs.

I remember in my earliest days at the bank I would wake up every morning in my Kilburn flat, look in the mirror and feel completely hollow. It was as if I had imploded during the night and only my skin remained. I would splash cold water on my face, even slap myself to try to generate some feeling, but if I felt anything it was just a vague sickness. I would get through my days with gallons of coffee and my nights with video games, reruns of *The Simpsons* and even larger quantities of alcohol. Perhaps, upon reflection, that accounts for my morning nausea.

When I moved to New York, I found a new group of friends and a new and exciting nightlife, and I was earning a lot more money. So I found myself going out almost every night of the week, often until two or three in the morning, dragging myself through work with increasing quantities of caffeine, and sleeping through the weekends without much thought. I had a lot of fun for a while. The empty feeling even went away sometimes. But it always returned sooner or later, on the rare occasions when I was sober and had a bit of time to think. On those occasions I

tainted

despised myself.

    A banker was the last thing in life I had wanted to become. When I was a child, after the fantasy of being a professional footballer had worn off, it was always a writer that I wanted to be. In taking the job at Citigroup, I'd even thought that I would be able to get home in the evenings and write my first book. It never happened, of course. I had failed to realize how deeply I would be affected by what I did all day every day. I had failed to realize that I would start to become a banker, no matter how much I tried to cut myself off from that horrific possibility. I was immersed in it. I was lying all day every day, pretending to be an ambitious young "rising star" who wanted nothing more than to be a senior vice president of insurance sales or a managing director of fund administration.

    At some point in the chaotic, blurred progress of my New York life, I remembered what I was supposed to be doing with my life. After a three-year haze of parties, pubs and clubs, I started cutting back on the drinking and the late nights, and I began to write again. It was excruciatingly hard. Whereas in my teens I could dash off a short story in an hour or two, I now found myself struggling for days and nights at a stretch just to get something I was reasonably happy with. Were my standards higher now, or had my brain turned to mush from all the alcohol and credit derivatives? I couldn't tell, but it terrified me. I decided that part-time writing was not enough: I needed to be doing it day in, day out. So I went to Columbia's Graduate School of Journalism, did a one-year Master's degree, and on graduation I landed a job at The Wall Street Journal.

    The Wall Street Journal, however, was not at all what I thought it would be. I had expected an *All the President's Men* brand of newsroom, with gritty reporters and editors cranking out hard-hitting investigative stories and trying to get to the truth. Instead I found a kind of "Citigroup lite." I was writing about personal finance - hardly what I had dreamed of - but it was a job, and I was writing, and that was all that seemed to matter.

    Many colleagues seemed more concerned about snappy headlines and cute anecdotes than tackling hard issues. Internal politics were rife, different sections of the paper squabbled over turf and bad ideas from favoured reporters got more play than good ideas from the uninitiated. And the executives paid themselves

quarter passed

millions of dollars in bonuses and stock options while telling the rank-and-file employees to accept another year of zero wage increases, "for the good of the company."

I suppose I was naïve to expect anything else. After all, a newspaper is a company like any other; its aim is to make money. When I got settled there, I started working on a novel in my spare time - between 5:30 am and 7:30 am every morning before work. Despite the pain of such an early start, it actually worked, and the chapters started coming together.

Nevertheless, my moonlighting as a novelist didn't change the fact that I spent my long hard work weeks writing fluff pieces. What disappointed me most of all was how this false advertising as a real news source affected the news coverage itself. Even in just the three years I was there, a noticeable shift took place towards advertiser-friendly "lifestyle" feature stories and away from hard news. And the stories were all aimed at rich people, because rich people can afford to buy the advertised Jaguars and Tiffany necklaces boxing in the articles. It was all very dispiriting. I had ended up back in the heart of Corporate America, except that I was earning a quarter of what I'd made at Citigroup and was working harder. Yes, I was writing, but it was not the kind of writing that I wanted to do. So I quit - again.

At this stage of my life the overwhelming feeling is uncertainty and a healthy amount of fear. What if my novel doesn't get published? What if it's no good? What if I'm just not as good a writer as I thought I was? Sometimes I am tempted to just revert to my old sedated self. Would that be so bad? After all, the last few years of living in reality rather than denial have not achieved much other than depleting my bank account and giving me some grey hair. Maybe denial is not such a bad thing. Besides, my friends at Citigroup certainly seemed happy enough most of the time, just earning lots of money and then blowing it on expensive restaurants and luxury vacations. I suspect that many of them had the same doubts that I did, but maybe - if those doubts were suppressed for long enough - they would just die away in the end? The booze would certainly kill any conscience that I have.

These are the questions that dog me as my twenties draw to a close. I am

tainted

still hopeful of finding a way to live that will satisfy me, but I haven't yet. I seem to have taken a very round-about route, but I have discovered what I want to be when I grow up - the writer that I knew was in me since I was a child.

andrew blackman. (29, beckenham, englamd)

quarter passed

off to work. by patrick emery yurick. (22, farmington, new hampshire, usa)

the first quarter
by brandon miree

A few years ago, "normal" to me was running full-speed towards another human being that was charging full throttle back at me.

"Low man wins..."

"A knee bender is a jaw breaker..."

They call this blocking. If you're dizzy when you walk back to the huddle, you hope that the man you blocked is too. If he is, you call that a good block. If a teammate gives you an "atta boy" slap on the head and you get a headache, you call that a good teammate. If you do this twenty to thirty times on a Sunday afternoon, you call that a good game. In America, they call this football, and if you love it, you call this a good dream.

The best players block, scrape and stomp to play in the National Football League. In America, football is a game of high salaries, higher stakes and the highest tension, but also extreme determination, devotion and passion. While you're playing, your body calls this pure adrenaline. When you're done, your mind calls it pure insanity.

Growing up, no one told me to love football. It was just something inside of me - God's gift to an otherwise ordinary boy. When I was a kid, I remember watching a game one day and almost coming to tears because I thought I didn't have big enough shoulders to play. I was too young to know they were wearing shoulder pads. What's more, I was too naïve to know how much more mental strength it would take to endure the hits than physical size.

A local businessman in my hometown of Cincinnati once challenged my sixth grade class to write down our goals and describe how we would achieve them - a cash prize to the winner. I composed an entire essay about "my vision of becoming a professional football player." I detailed a step-by-step plan starting that upcoming summer all the way through being drafted after college graduation. I won the cash prize and I began a long journey to fulfilling my mission.

My dream started to become a reality in seventh grade, the first time I had a chance to play running back. Until that point, my modest stature had relegated me to spots on the offensive line. But a well-timed growth spurt and a rigorous training regimen endowed me with uncommon strength, speed and size. I grew up idolizing backfield stars like Walter Payton, so it was with some pride that I took the field that day. I ran for eight yards on the first play of the game. On the second play, I ran for a touchdown which, unfortunately, was called back because of a penalty on my team. On the third play, I ran for a touchdown again. By the time the game was over, I had trounced up and down the turf for five touchdowns.

That's not to say that my successes came without failures. When, as a ninth grader, I took the field for our varsity team's first scrimmage - which, incidentally, was against all-everything Shaun Alexander's alma mater, Boone County - the speed of the game was too fast. Even though I had the necessary size and speed, my mind couldn't handle the different defensive schemes, and I fumbled the ball my first two plays. I was ineffective and humiliated because I was simply not ready to play varsity football. My high school coach, who was a real leader and mentor, told me that he didn't want to see me struggle; he wanted me to be a star. So he pulled me back to play with my fellow freshmen. After that restart, I rushed for two touchdowns against mighty Moeller and eventually won team MVP.

The next year presented me with another challenge. I was ready to play varsity football and explode onto Cincinnati's sports scene. Hours before the first game of the season, I was talking to my brother and neighbor about gearing up and preparing to run out onto the field. I told them that I never tape my ankles - and I remember them telling me to make sure that I do. I wish I had. During the first play, a lineman rolled over my ankle on a chop block. I was out the rest of the game, unable to even walk. I missed game after game while the season advanced without me.

My first game back was against our rival, the Harrison Wildcats. By that time, our team already had an emerging star in senior transfer running back, Keith Brooks. Coming off the bench, I lined up in a two-point stance in the backfield.

the first quarter

As the quarterback made his calls, the defense adjusted their positioning.

"Set hut!"

I took a hand-off from the quarterback and began to run up field. The night air was cold, and I wasn't wearing any gloves. The chill was biting at my fingertips and, before I knew it, the ball started to slip out of my hands - and I fumbled. The other team jumped on the ball. I trotted back to the sidelines with my head hung low. Great first play in a varsity football game. I was not exactly becoming the pro that I wrote about years before.

After that fumble I hardly played another down on offense for the rest of the game. When the occasion to redeem myself finally arose, it was only because Keith was doing so well that everyone in the stadium knew he was going to get the ball - and we needed a distraction. My coach gave me another chance. I found myself in the huddle glancing around at the senior linemen who didn't want to see me there. Keith walked into the huddle with a serious look on his face and said, "28 sweep and DON'T FUMBLE THE BALL."

His look said it all. He wanted to win and didn't want some unproven, over-hyped sophomore to mess it up for him. There was no margin for error. I knew that no matter what, I would not let the ball get loose from my grip. I took the sweep, ran around the corner, and was tackled after about ten yards. As I stood up, I immediately felt a deep pain in my ankle.

I got up and limped back to the bench where I watched the rest of the game as the Keith Brooks show went primetime. I was once told that there is no progress without struggle. On the injured list for the rest of the season, I drifted into obscurity, but I was not yet defeated.

Junior year came, a breakout season when I finally put the pieces together, taped my ankles religiously and I rushed for over 1,000 yards in a crowded backfield. Senior year was more of the same, and I ran for 2,455 yards. At last, I had become the player that I wanted to be. Yet, it still felt like I didn't get as much respect in local circles as I should have. Instead, two other glorified district running backs - both of whom had already committed to play college ball for the pride of all eighty-eight counties, Ohio State - got all the press and accolades.

quarter passed

Nonetheless, colleges came knocking on my door. I chose the University of Alabama over Michigan State University, the University of Notre Dame, Boston College and the University of Pittsburgh.

The running back I had been brought in to succeed, all-everything Shaun Alexander, was already making waves at 'Bama by the time I arrived. Needless to say, I spent my first three years with the Crimson Tide acquiring a Southern accent and watching games from the bench.

Prior to my third year at 'Bama, I made the decision to transfer to the University of Pittsburgh. My tenure at Pitt was a great success. Given the chance to showcase my talents on the gridiron, I scored a game-capping fifty-five yard touchdown run to lead our team to an upset over Virginia Tech, the third-ranked team in the country. I went on to earn offensive player of the game honors at the Insight Bowl and, after a senior season of ups and downs, I was claimed by the Denver Broncos in the seventh round of the NFL Draft.

In football, like life, as soon as you're born you begin to die. From the moment you're drafted, your days are numbered. You could be a first round pick, but on the first day of the first season on the first play of the game, it could all be over in an instant. The average career of an NFL player is just three and a half seasons. Those who play my position, blocking and running the ball, have an even a shorter professional lifespan. I knew that when I began playing this sport. The clock is always ticking, asking you when enough is enough. But, I came to play.

The Denver Broncos were known for a relentless, punishing brand of running the ball and since the team roster was already overcrowded, I spent my first year in the NFL on the injured reserved list. In the offseason, I kept in shape by playing in NFL Europe, but when I came back to Denver for my second season, the team was still too deep in the backfield, and I was consigned to being a backup's backup.

Our coaches stressed the importance of oneness and they seamlessly integrated new players into the team. We running backs were constantly together - to support, encourage, and teach one another. But the fierce competition kept us sharp and constantly improving. I adopted a mindset of unity with my teammates

the first quarter

and, instead of sinking into complacency, I kept working and learning and waiting for my chance.

Then, a light shined on September 7th, 2006 when I got a phone call from the Green Bay Packers. Mike McCarthy, the team's rookie head coach, had adopted a running scheme similar to the one employed by the Broncos. Most of the Packers' personnel were unfamiliar with the new system, and the coaches felt that I could come in and make an impact right away. I got the call at noon, and by 4:00 pm, I was on a flight to Green Bay, Wisconsin. I arrived at the Austin Straubel International Airport around 6:30 am and was shuttled straight to the stadium.

Physical... equipment... practice... roster. It happened that fast.

I didn't feel comfortable in my equipment that first day, and I was exhausted from the spontaneity of this career switch. Changing cities, companies and jobs in a day isn't easy in any industry. But, this is the NFL. Coaches and scouts want to see how much skill and heart you have. It's all part of the business. You have to start over and prove why you belong each time you join a new team; you have to earn your spot. The coaches put me on the scout team, against the first team defense, to see what I brought with me.

That initial practice was a blur. It was an average day at best for me, but I did get a few slaps on the head when I made a great block on first-round draft pick A.J. Hawk.

Two days later, after a few nights of good sleep, I had recovered and was ready to work. More eyeballs locked on to me as I went into my stride and began to make my mark. I knew I had done something right when Brett Favre finally spoke to me. Guys have this macho way of acknowledging you. For some, the gesture is a slap on the head or, occasionally, on the butt; others may brag about you to another teammate. For Brett, it was a simple question.

"Was you at Alabama when the strength coach Ken was there?" He didn't have to say anything else; I knew that was his way of accepting me. He was building a rapport with somebody who could help bring the team to victory.

The offensive coordinator told me that as soon as I learned the offense, I would move up to the active squad. I worked dutifully to internalize the playbook, spending early mornings and late evenings poring over the system and checks.

quarter passed

By the time I got my bearings, the season was already underway and the early games I watched were brutal. We lost our first home game against the Chicago Bears, 29-0. The team was in a rebuilding phase when I was hired, and the fact that we were the youngest team in the league (with the oldest starting quarterback) wasn't to our advantage.

I just kept pushing and waiting for my time to shine until, at last, they put me on the first team at practice. I ran a play at one of the hardest hitting linebackers on the team. When I knocked him down, the other players went wild. Talk about getting kudos! More slaps on the head ensued.

Aaron Rodgers, Green Bay's second-string quarterback at the time, pulled me aside one day and complimented me. He told me I was doing well, and that if I kept doing so, I would end up being a starter. He also told me that if I didn't keep up the pace, I would spiral down into oblivion. I took those words to heart and held them close. I wanted to be "the guy" instead of "a guy." In the NFL, if you're not standing out, you are not around for long.

After a dismal running performance in the team's third season game, I was told to get ready. My position coach told me that they were going to find a spot for me to play when we faced the Philadelphia Eagles the next Monday night.

I was announced as the starter on the Thursday before the game amid a lot of media publicity. The former starter, Will Henderson, was a Pro Bowl fullback and one of the few team members left from the franchise's Super Bowl victory a decade before. This occasion also marked my introduction to the media spotlight. Not really aware of what the fuss was about, and not used to all the cameras in my face, I stumbled over my response to a relatively simple question:

"What is it about your knowledge of the West Coast blocking scheme that makes you valuable at that position?"

My answer lacked the humility with which I was raised, and that hindsight brought me.

"I'm just good at being able to read the hole like a running back; I'm just good." I still shake my head and laugh whenever I think back to the overconfidence and naiveté of that statement.

In my hotel room, I got calls from an endless stream of family members and

the first quarter

friends who had heard the news on ESPN. I didn't even know that many people had my number. I had spent my whole life working to become a professional football player, and my endeavors were going to be realized in less than twenty-four hours. I felt resolved to stay on top of the mountain for as long as possible. After all, I hadn't just walked into the league yesterday. I had been paying my dues since day one, fighting an uphill battle through ten running backs in Denver and the minor leagues in Europe, and living with the constant awareness that I could be cut at any moment. Through it all, I kept perspective, kept persevering, and now I would finally have my name lit up on the big board.

Game day is all about anticipation. The silence can be paralyzing. I rolled out of bed focused, not nervous, yet I was anxious for the first snap. Monday Night games are special, almost ceremonial, and can take an eternity to begin. I kept running plays over and over in my mind. Philly's blitz-heavy defense sends players all over the field at the opposing offense with one swarming intention in mind - disrupt everything.

As we pulled into the stadium on our team bus, the feeling was electric; this was The City of Brotherly Love on a Monday night. We would be surrounded by some of the most fanatic spectators in the world. In a few short hours, they would be hurling beer bottles and cussing our mothers to their delight.

I remembered the sage words of my old coach at 'Bama, "Football is played between the lines." If we just concentrated on what we had to do, everything else would take care of itself. We didn't have to play against 55,000 rabid screaming onlookers; rather, we had a group of fifty-three guys on the other side of the field with whom we needed to concern ourselves.

As I dressed for pre-game, the special teams coach walked over to inform me that I would be playing on kickoffs and kickoff returns in addition to my starting role on offense. There was only one problem: I hadn't done this before. No practice, no nothing. My week had consisted of preparing to play fullback, not memorizing how to backpedal down the field while positioning myself to block an opponent who's running at me with the sole purpose of laying me flat on the ground.

My psychological edge was thrown off by having to mentally prepare for a new role just minutes before kickoff. Despite that, because I was committed to being "the guy," I headed out onto the field early to receive some last-minute coaching and to practice catching kickoffs that spiraled down at me from ninety feet in the air.

In the locker room, before a game, some players are mellow; some sniff smelling sauce and make loud noises; some zone out with their headphones. I hovered somewhere in between. I clenched my mouthpiece as we knelt down for a prayer; the rumbles of the crowd roared in the seats above the locker room. Amen.

In the tunnel, I stood in the back of the offense, mouthpiece in place, hands at my sides and legs crossed. I breathed steadily and relaxed my muscles. I was ready. The announcer introduced our team as we ran onto the field. Relentless boos rained down from the crowd. I ran in place as the announcer summoned our defensive personnel. This was what it's all about. Hand slaps ensued. Coin toss.

We got the ball first. I was up on kickoff. Great, now I could show off all of that pre-game practice. We galloped onto the field. The Eagles lined-up and I squatted in my stance. The ball was kicked, and I sprinted back to my position. I turned around and looked for my man, the target I was supposed to knock down. Where was he?

The first rule on kickoffs is that when you lose your designated adversary, you go to the next. My rationale and training were lost in the bright lights; I kept looking for my mark. Wrong move. Suddenly and fortuitously, he appeared; I sighed in relief and pinned my entire body on top of his before our kick returner was tackled.

The offense ran out onto the field. "Regular!" That meant that I was on the field. We huddled up. Brett Favre stepped in.

"I right 27 Buster, ready... Break." We lined up on the ball. This was a play that I had run a million times.

"Set Hut!"

I ran straight for the outside linebacker as fast and as low as I could. I used my forearm and ripped it right into his chest, my forehead at his numbers. Perfect block. His heels dragged in the ground as I drove him back so far that the only thing that kept him from falling was his teammate. As I walked back to the

the first quarter

huddle, I looked back at him and his eyes said it all; I would own him the entire game.

We gained seven yards on the play. The offense got one first down before we had to kick. When we got the ball back, a long play put us close to their end zone, only twenty-five yards out. On second down and eight, they called my first pass play.

As Brett hiked the ball, I ran out of the backfield and turned to look for the pass. I've played with many quarterbacks in my career, several of whom had a rocket arm. The difference between playing with other quarterbacks and playing with Brett was touch. It's one thing to be able to get the ball to your receiver and to thread the needle. It's quite another thing to know how to perfectly place the ball into your receiver's hands. Brett's passes never felt heavy.

Unfortunately, as he threw this particular ball, I misjudged the distance between us. The ball hit me in the face and bounced into the sky. Time froze for a moment. I snatched it out of the air, planted, pivoted and sprinted upfield. I got tackled near the sidelines for a first down.

The head slaps told me that it had been a great play, but I knew that my brother would never let me hear the end of the bobbled catch. I could already hear him saying, "Nice catch, Brandon. First time you've used your head in years."

Still, the entire day was a solid effort. Even though we lost, I lived to start another day.

As each game progressed, I got better and more comfortable at my position. I was emerging as a new young talent. My breakout game came against the Arizona Cardinals. But just as quickly as I amassed forty yards in catches, the game turned on me. Actually, to be precise, it turned on my arm. A hyper-extended elbow can really ruin your Sunday.

When I recovered from the injury three weeks later, I was no longer a starter. I was sharing duties and being worked back into regular play. Even so, we ended up winning four of our last five games and capped off the season with a victory over the Chicago Bears, barely missing the playoffs.

The offseason had a lot of positives to build on, and it became apparent that I was going to be "the guy." The team had released their long-time starting

quarter passed

fullback and didn't sign any veterans to take my place. My position coach constantly programmed me to think Pro Bowl and nothing less, and I worked tirelessly to become the best fullback in the league. I knew that I would be a restricted free agent after the season, which only strengthened my resolve to have a defining season - after four hard years.

When training camp started, I got off on the right foot. Newspaper articles were written about me being back to my full form. I got encouragement and respect from my coaches and the front office and plenty of head slaps from teammates. My position coach told me that everything I was doing was positive. Until I got hurt again.

In football, injury can mean death and a slow recovery can drive nails into your coffin. I missed two weeks of training camp. When you consider that one day of training camp packs in three to four days of information and drills, two weeks is a significant amount of time.

Everyone started looking at me differently. I saw something behind the glances that they gave when I walked by. Eyes lingered just long enough to register recognition before darting on. I began to ask myself, "Am I losing confidence or are they?" Honestly, I couldn't tell anymore.

As I soaked and recovered on the sidelines, the offensive masterminds experimented and figured out how to utilize me less and less by employing a more spread-out offensive system. One minor systematic change and a player becomes expendable.

One fateful day, two weeks later, I got a phone call from the front office saying that the Green Bay Packers had decided to "part ways with me."

I returned to the team facilities one last time to fill out some paperwork and clean out my locker. As I pulled out old socks, shoes and gloves and crammed them into an oversized black trash bag, Brett Favre walked into the room. I could tell he'd witnessed this scene many times before. He walked up and gave me a big hug.

"We'll miss ya," he said.

"Right back at ya," I replied. "Go out there and do well this year."

He nodded humbly in approval and walked out of the room. As I stood there

the first quarter

in silence, it was as if my entire career flashed before my eyes. This was the end of my football life, the first quarter of my existence on Earth.

I try to never limit myself by doing just one thing. As a student-athlete at 'Bama and Pitt, I earned a bachelors degree in Public Administration, took graduate-level courses, and adopted screenwriting and filmmaking as hobbies. As an NFL player, I worked with inner city kids and took on a larger role in my community.

Retiring at twenty-six was never an option (nor an attraction) for me. The second quarter is just getting underway, and I find myself working just as hard as I did during my years as a professional athlete. I'm currently producing a major motion picture; my record label is releasing a major hip hop compilation album; and I continually travel as a motivational speaker using music and sports to reach young people.

In spite of these accomplishments, I constantly encounter new setbacks and hurdles. However, the education I received on the gridiron has taught me the value of purpose and a positive mental attitude, and I am excited for what the future may bring.

When the clock runs out on the first quarter, there is still plenty of game left to play.

brandon miree. (27, cincinnati, ohio, usa)

About Twenty Stories Publishing

Twenty Stories Publishing was founded in 2007 as an independent publishing company - an alternative to conventional publishing - and is dedicated to the promotion of young authors, artists, poets and photographers from all walks of life. Through an interactive publishing process, Twenty Stories Publishing enables young adults to share ideas, experiences and creative expression with a global audience.

To learn more about Twenty Stories Publishing, or to submit your own creative works for publication, visit www.twentystories.com.

Printed in the United States
141463LV00003B/13/P